KENTON, BRANTON

QUANTUM C

D1580765

QUANTUM CARROT

Branton Kenton

EBURY PRESS · LONDON

For

Fred Mathias and George Thomas

635. 048

Published by Ebury Press
Division of The National Magazine Company Ltd
Colquhoun House, 27–37 Broadwick Street, London W1V 1FR

First impression 1987

ISBN 0 85223 589 5

Edited by Suzanne Webber and Gillian Haslam
Designed by Gwyn Lewis
Illustrations by Ted McCausland/Ron Haywood
Cover illustration by Cathy Wood

Computerset in Great Britain by MFK Typesetting Ltd, Hitchin, Herts

Printed in Great Britain at The Bath Press, Bath, Avon

Illustrations on pages 135–137 reprinted by permission of
Faber and Faber Ltd from *Vegetables from Small Gardens* by
Joy Larkcom, illustrations by Elizabeth Winson

Contents

Acknowledgements

Without the generosity of many farmers and growers from Pembrokeshire I could not have begun to grow organically. In particular I am indebted to Fred Mathias, George Thomas and Cliff Griffiths, to whom I apologize for the late return of his potato swipe. I thank all the many people who have shared their time and knowledge with me on my land, especially Mal, Jonny and Peter, who often worked harder with me than they thought possible. All members of the British organic movement, in particular Charlie and Caroline Watcher, who gave me such sound practical advice and encouragement, have been an inspiration to me. Plas Dwbl farm, tucked under the Preseli mountains, is a constant reminder of the richness that can be ours. Many thanks to everyone at Cornelyn Manor for their friendship and support while I wrote. Finally, my thanks to my mother, Leslie Kenton, for gathering research papers and for advice on how to structure this book.

Foreword by Leslie Kenton

This is a truly revolutionary book. It takes the discoveries of some of the world's finest scientific minds and translates them into living practical realities. It gives each of us who reads it the chance to put into practice the visionary science with its view of a unified world—a world in which man's choice plays a key role in determining both our individual and our collective future. So seldom does one come across a book written by someone who has both an understanding of leading edge theories and the practical skills necessary to use them—in this case to use them not only as a means of heightening our own health and vitality but of improving the health of our Earth. In a unique way *Quantum Carrot* fulfils two very important roles: it is an easily understood map of the new consciousness as well as a 'nuts and bolts' guide to putting it into practice through small space organic gardening.

Following in the wake of the 'new physics', the latest theories of leading edge scientists are shaking traditional assumptions about reality and about the nature of man's power to their very core. It is a trembling which has already begun to affect the lives of every one of us—some say more like an earthquake, the reverberations from which will echo down through the 21st century.

Since Greek times our scientists and philosophers have assumed that there is a split between man and the world around him, between spirit and matter. This belief was powerfully reinforced by the theories of Newton and Descartes whose work created the scientific and philosophical paradigms on which our modern sense of reality is based. And such paradigms are a great deal more than just a useful theoretical model for science. Their philosophical implications infiltrate the minds of us all and have powerful influences on society and its values whether or not we have even heard of the scientific research and theories on which they are based.

The Cartesian-Newtonian paradigm with which we and our ancestors have lived for generations has resulted in a very negative view of man. It is a view which depicts him as fundamentally impotent—

powerless to influence his own destiny and the destiny of our earth. He has been seen as a biological machine driven by instinctual impulses which are fundamentally destructive in nature and which need to be kept in check. This 'old world' view has also encouraged us to look upon life as an ultimately futile process—an accidental occurence within an endless struggle to maintain order and thus postpone death.

But since the turn of the century, and particularly in the past 20 years, the notion of a separation between mind and matter, between the objective world and the subject who observes it has been nothing less than completely exploded by relativity theory, quantum physics and the new biology. Leading edge scientists have discovered that order is not, as we have been taught to believe, a static state against which we must constantly struggle to survive but a dynamic process of energy exchange between the living body and the world outside and that consciousness itself plays an important part in both the creation of living organisms and in carrying out living processes.

We will never again be able to speak about the universe without speaking about ourselves in the same breath. For suddenly, after thousands of years of seeing otherwise, matter is no longer static, made up of passive building blocks. It consists of active bundles of energy continuously involved in dynamic processes. And consciousness, far from being a result of the material world, now appears to play a primary creative role in creating it.

The implications of such a paradigm shift are earthshaking. For it is becoming clear that we as human beings can influence the primary realms of reality and choose the direction of our future evolution. Man is emerging as a creator in his own right—someone able to experience the leading edge scientist's vision of wholeness as a living reality and in doing so to help create his own future and the future of our planet.

Branton Kenton suggests that small space organic growing of foods—so simple that a complete amateur can practise it even in the kitchen of a city flat—is a powerful tool for doing both. *Quantum Carrot* shows the reader in remarkably clear and simple ways how and why. Here is a book which quite literally inspired me as well as introducing me to the techniques of organic food growing of which I had little knowledge. I was delighted to be asked to write a foreword to it. And since Branton Kenton also happens to be my eldest son, it brought home to me yet again just how very much we all have to learn from our children.

Introduction

At the edge of darkness

Life in today's world presents serious problems. Every day we are bombarded with new forms of environmental pollution that fill our air, contaminate our water, and taint the food we eat. Pesticides, industrial waste, food additives and radiation can all take their toll on our health and vitality. Pesticide residues find their way into the flesh of unborn children and contaminate the mother's milk. In the United States the American National Cancer Institute has predicted that one in three children will develop cancer during their lifetimes. A healthy body could counter these harmful influences, but high quality, fresh organic foods which can provide the quality of nutrition necessary to create such a high level of health are only available to a small minority of the population, and often at exorbitant prices. For many this has meant a life of lack-lustre health, rapid degeneration, and the constant threat of disease.

No less frightening is the many faceted crisis facing the very existence of life on this planet. We no longer need a nuclear war to end all life as we know it. British scientist, Jim Lovelock warns that many of the Earth's vital life support systems may be on the brink of breakdown through man's destruction of the planet's ecology. Without these systems, which provide essential oxygen, carbon dioxide, and temperature control, life would cease.

To many these problems seem insoluble. After all, how do you keep track of every one of the 6,000 new chemicals registered in the United States each week, let alone worry about whether your supermarket vegetables have been irradiated to increase their shelf life? After the complexities of just surviving the modern world, it can even seem a matter of indifference whether we destroy ourselves through nuclear war, or the breakdown of planetary ecology. Often facing up to the realities of modern life only fills us with anger, frustration or despair, because we feel powerless to do anything about them.

Quantum Carrot suggests that these and other problems are not insoluble, but are in fact the opportunity for creating a new kind of wealth based on personal health, vitality, individual power and autonomy. Unlike the conventional notion of wealth—two cars and a house in the country—this new wealth is available to everyone. Of course there is nothing wrong with the house in the country, but a now measurable shift in values suggests that, unlike the material affluence of the 50's, or the pleasure seeking 60's, the new wealth of the 80's and 90's will be firmly grounded in a sense of health and well-being.

The contribution of organic gardening

Quantum Carrot can make a major contribution to this new wealth through small space organic gardening. What few people realize is that they can grow an abundance of organic food for themselves and their families in a few square feet of garden, in window boxes, or even in flower pots at home. *Quantum Carrot* describes the latest, simplest, most effective and enjoyable growing techniques. Freshly harvested organic vegetables, uncontaminated by toxic pesticide residues, are one of the best sources of high level nourishment available anywhere, at any price. They are acknowledged by leading health foundations and cancer help centres as powerful protection against environmental pollution—a passport to long lasting health. They can be grown with the minimum of time or space, and are remarkably inexpensive—cheaper than lower quality supermarket foods.

More remarkable still is the fact that by the very process of creating this high level health-based wealth, at the same time one is working on many fronts to heal the Earth. For instance, organic gardening depends on making the most of the countless millions of soil organisms from microscopic bacteria and fungi to worms. They provide the right nutrients at the right time to ensure strong healthy growth. At the same time they are an intricate part of the Earth's life support systems. By increasing the health of plants, the Earth is strengthened. For perhaps the first time in history, our needs are also the needs of the planet: they have become one.

However, it would be foolish to pretend that a couple of lettuce grown in the living room are going to change our lives overnight, let alone solve any facet of the global crisis that faces us. What possible use is it, you may ask, to know that the few herbs I grow are organic, when I must buy the rest of my food, complete with pesticide residues, growth hormones, etc? Or how can the biological activity of my small patch of garden compensate for the one hundred acres of rainforest destroyed every minute? Certainly, if the *Quantum Carrot* approach was just a guide on how to grow lettuce and tomatoes, there would be no grounds for hope. Thankfully, history seems to show that out of every crisis comes a solution.

The Quantum Link

This book is called *Quantum Carrot* because it is about a unique marriage between the revolutionary implications of quantum physics and the down-to-earth practice of growing your own foods. It is a book which combines visions of reality now emerging at the leading edge of science with simple practices. What after all could be more humble than the carrot? *Quantum Carrot* is all about a new way of increasing your own health and vitality while expanding your consciousness, quite literally to transform the world we live in. Unlikely as it may seem, the suggestion is that the linkup between the findings of quantum physics and practical small space organic gardening creates within us the power for positive change. I have called it the Quantum Link. The challenge of *Quantum Carrot* is to forge that link for ourselves.

This may sound a little far-fetched. That is certainly what I thought until I started to feel the power of the link in my own life. Consider for a moment how good you would feel if, instead of being at the mercy of the destructive forces around us, you stood at the centre of things, in control, your thoughts and actions making the life you want. Consider what would happen if increased personal health and vitality had consequences beyond just feeling fit and looking good. And what if your small plot of land or window box had the power to heal the Earth far greater than its size would suggest? These are the bold possibilities quantum physical research presents when combined with practical small scale organic gardening.

Bold yes, but not a pipe-dream. Already in other fields, the insights of quantum physics are positively changing our lives. For instance psychiatrist Dorothy Rowe has used these findings to create a new understanding of psychological problems, while American writer Joseph Chilton Pearce has begun to transform our understanding of how we grow up in his books *Magical Child* and *Magical Child Matures*. What all these new approaches have in common is the belief in the power of the individual to create the well-being that is no more than his or her genetic inheritance.

For us living on the Earth at this difficult time, the way to this new personal wealth rests on each of us making a unique choice. This choice faces us as the result of the pace of change in the world today. Change is now so fast that the only thing for certain is that nothing will stay the same. Many of the signs of change, from the daily addition to the 33,000 chemicals already in common use to the speed we are cutting down the remaining virgin rainforest, indicate that the old ways we have gone about things no longer work as they used to, and are leading us into serious problems in terms of health and environmental collapse. The choice we are faced with is whether we continue with these old outdated habit patterns and accept things are going to get worse, or see it as an opportunity to create a life we want to live.

The *Quantum Carrot* approach says yes to this opportunity and, in its own way through small space organic gardening, begins to grow that new wealth. It is a wealth which until now, without the new insight into our creative power and potential suggested by quantum physical research, or the possibilities opened to us by the pace of change in the world, would not have been possible. The challenge of *Quantum Carrot* is to buy a packet of seeds and see for yourself. Faced with today's problems, our only option is to respond to the pace of change or perish. This is the adventure of our lifetime.

The Quantum Carrot Adventure

The Goal
A new wealth based on health, personal power and autonomy, for you and the Earth, through small space organic gardening

What are you playing against?
★　Fear　★　Feelings of powerlessness　★　Dangerous die-hard habits

What do you need to get started?
★　A desire to change　★　Information　★　A packet of seeds
★　Any small plot of land, a window box, or even just a few flower pots

What are your challenges?
★　Lack-lustre health　★　A pollution-filled environment ★　A false sense of dependence on low quality supermarket foods

How to win:
★　Understanding the Quantum Link

PART ONE - EARTHCRISIS

ONE

At The Leading Edge of Change

Few people realize the speed of change in their world today. And that speed is accelerating at each step. For instance, it took one million years for the first billion human beings to inhabit the Earth, one hundred years for the next, and probably 15 years for the next. This rate of change is exponential, that is to say, the pace quickens with every step—like the growth of yogurt culture where the first cell divides into two, both of those divide creating 4, 4 to 8, 8 to 16, 16 to 32, 32 to 64 . . . and so on. Such a devastating pace of change has important consequences for us because it is profoundly altering the world we live in. In order to come to terms with that world, and to live in it at the peak of our potential, we need to understand the nature of change so that we can use its unique possibilities to our own advantage.

Graphs of exponential change are easy to identify by their steeply rising curves like the following examples. One feature all graphs of exponential change have in common is that as the gradient gets steeper, it becomes impossible any longer to predict accurately the changes that are taking place—at the top of the curve we enter the unknown. Perhaps it is this sense of the unknown that is the most intimidating, but also the most exciting aspect of our changing world.

Scientists (many of them Nobel Prize winners), politicians, farmers and university professors are waking up to the fact that this accelerating pace of change is creating new pressures on ourselves and the world—pressures never experienced before. In Africa, a population of half a billion is already putting unbearable burdens on the political, social, and ecological systems, triggering wars, famine, the breakup of culture, and rapid advance of the desert. If the present growth rate of 3% a year continues, what will the situation be like this time next century with a population of 9.5 billion?

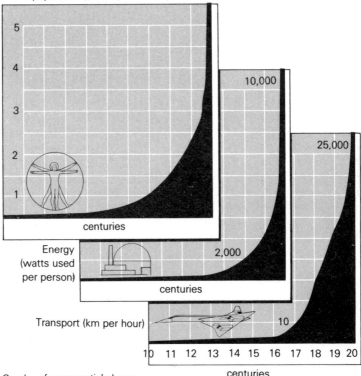

World population (billions)

5
4
3
2
1

centuries

10,000

2,000

25,000

Energy
(watts used
per person)

centuries

Transport (km per hour)

10

10 11 12 13 14 15 16 17 18 19 20

centuries

Graphs of exponential change

In order to master these new problems created by the pace of change we need radical new solutions which can only grow out of creative and imaginative ways of thinking and activity. This accelerating pace of change has brought us face to face with problems never experienced before, for instance, in the screening of food additives. We know in some detail the harmful effects of some individual food additives through toxicological experiments. This helped us when the number of food additives was small, but now, with the increasing number of permitted additives, these experiments are no longer accurate guides to the potential harm done to us when we eat additive-filled foods. Why? Because they give no indication of the new dangers the additives may pose when combined. The pace of change means it is practically impossible to know the harm of eating such food. Faced with new problems like this, how do we solve them?

The changing of the shrew

Many people have responded to the new challenge of multiple additives in food by eliminating those foods as far as possible from their diets—a creative solution to a new problem. But for most of us such changes cannot occur overnight. If, like me, you are a creature of habit, you may prefer stability to change, and security rather than the unknown. Konrad Lorenz, the famous observer of animal behaviour, describes this attitude beautifully in his humorous account of how shrews deal with change.

In *King Solomon's Ring*, Lorenz explains that, like most of us, shrews are creatures of habit. What's more they have such a high metabolic rate that they have to eat every few hours to stop them from starving, and are incredibly short sighted.

Lorenz kept a colony in a glass tank so he could observe their movements. At first they were very wary of their new home, moving cautiously, nose to the ground, uncertain and hesitant. But after a few days they could be seen rushing around at lightning speed.

Lorenz noticed they always kept to the same route in their tank. In particular, if they were disturbed away from their nestbox they always skirted the side of the pond, leapt onto a large rock, and from the rock onto the roof of the nest, tumbling into the entrance upside down. This they performed at high speed. Then one day Lorenz removed the rock from the tank. A little while later he approached the tank. A shrew saw him and in top gear started to head for home, reaching the pond, skirting around its edge, leaping for the rock . . . only to land flat on its face! Bemused, the poor shrew picked itself up, shook its head, went back to the pond, skirted its edge and leapt again with the same result. Unable to continue the express route it knew so well it became slow and cautious again, and put its nose to the ground.

Change is the pulse of life

There are some very good reasons why many of us, like shrews, are creatures of habit. Habit provides the stability we need to build the lives we want. Every seed we plant needs good rich soil in which to germinate and grow, and will suffer if we dig it up every five minutes. Even the smallest lettuce seedling needs to put down roots if it is to grow a firm heart. At the same time, however, we sometimes lose sight of the fact that, besides stability, a lettuce plant also changes as it grows—from seed to seedling and to the first true leaves, supported by sun and rain, cycles of light and dark, and so forth. Preoccupied with holding on to what we have got, we can lose that sense of flow that is the natural course of things. One of the great benefits of organic gardening is that it gets us back into the rhythms of the seasons and the natural metamorphosis of all plants as they grow to maturity. Away from our usual day to day world where many people expend a great deal of effort just trying to maintain the status quo, a few minutes in the garden realigns you with the constantly changing activity of the greatest power on this planet—life itself. '*There is nothing constant in the universe*', wrote the philosopher Ovid more than 2,000 years ago. '*All ebb and flow, and every shape that's born, bears in its womb the seeds of change.*' By aligning ourselves like this to the life forces we can begin to harmonize with their energies to initiate the changes we want to see in ourselves and those around us. We will be working *with* the forces of change, using the possibilities presented by them to create the lives we choose. Sadly though, we often see change as our enemy rather than our friend, and resist its influence, preferring to stop where we are than enter the unknown.

Change? What change?

If you are anything like me you will find that the greatest single obstacle to change is yourself. Change can intimidate because we feel threatened by it, either because we don't think we will be able to cope, or because it will take away our sources of security—jobs, material possessions, partners, status—all the things that matter to us and make us feel 'safe'.

   People react in different ways. I tend to become impulsive, preferring action, any action, to the unknown. I know a director of a large company who becomes aggressive when threatened. 'Change', he bellows, 'don't talk to me about change. I've fought in two wars and I would have fought in the Falklands if they had let me go. What I don't know about change my son, isn't worth knowing.' Others go very quiet, hoping in some way that if they do not get themselves noticed, somehow change will pass them by—like an ostrich with its head stuck in the sand.

Victims or masters of change?

There are two problems with these reactions to change. The first is that they are techniques to *avoid* rather than to deal with the problem.

They are ways we shy away from the unknown, which means we miss the possibilities to initiate positive change, and get out of touch with the constant life-flow that may be the single most precious gift small space organic gardening has to offer. Avoidance makes us *victims* of change, rather than its masters. If we see the weeds germinating amongst our plants and do nothing about it, we will lose our crop. In the same way, if we are still eating the same way we did ten years ago, and continuing to ignore all the dangers of new processing methods and ways of improving shelf life with stabilizers, gums, radioactive bombardment and preservatives, we risk becoming victims of poor health, early ageing, and disease.

Sometimes we make all the right noises about changing, but deep down are hoping that if we talk about it enough we won't have to do anything. The sad thing about avoiding change is that it is the way to the poverty of the 8o's rather than its wealth. Why? Because in today's world it's impossible to stay where we are. The only choice we have is whether we ignore all the warning signals and continue the old ways of doing things that now lead us close to disaster, or whether we choose to understand that change is integral to the nature of things and then align ourselves with its potential to produce the kind of world and values we want to see. This is the difference between being a victim and a master of change.

To become masters of change in our daily lives is the aim of *Quantum Carrot*—using small space gardening to get us in tune with the power for positive change which ceaselessly flows through the Earth. But to make that choice I have found it useful to look at the reasons and ways I avoid change in my life. Then, even if I am still intimidated by the unknown, and become impulsive when confronted with something that threatens my nice secure habits, at least I am aware of what I am doing and can put my efforts into being the way I would rather be. You might like to try the same exercise yourself and see what you come up with. It will certainly be worthwhile because there are several patterns to our changing world which suggest we are just at the right time to create a new wealth on this planet which has never been possible before. Let's look at what those patterns are.

Enter the Sigmoid curve

One of the most fascinating patterns to emerge from the fast climbing graphs of exponential change has come from biologist Jonas Salk, inventor of the Salk polio vaccine, and now Director of the Salk Institute, La Jolla, California. Studying those high curves of change, Salk began to wonder what might be their eventual outcome. After all, if, for example, you took the population curve, it's obvious that we are fast approaching the maximum number of people our small planet can sustain, (most experts say 4 billion is nearing the limit). So what happens? Maybe Homo Sapiens has the same growth curve as lemmings, who every so often, when numbers get out of hand, show group behaviour that drastically reduces the population, namely they all throw themselves off the nearest cliff and die.

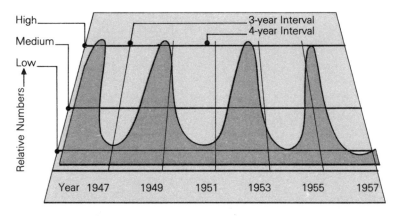

Generalised curve of the 3–4 year cycle of the brown lemming population

Are human beings like that? At times of population stress, do they respond to some group genetic coding and skillfully plan their own execution? Maybe that is what nuclear power or nuclear weapons, cutting down our oxygen supply, or mutagenic compounds in our food are all about—rather crude control mechanisms for our population.

Salk admits to the possibility, but prefers (who wouldn't) another solution. Looking again at biological systems, Salk found the 'lemming method' biologically unpopular. Instead, he discovered that many organisms regulate their populations in much subtler ways when they came up against factors limiting their growth. For instance, a yogurt culture will continue to grow exponentially until it starts to run out of one of the things it needs to continue its growth—food supply, oxygen, space, optimum temperature, etc. At that point a *qualitative* change take place in the graph. There is a change from progressive acceleration to progressive deceleration. The result is that the bacteria find their *optimum* population density in an ordered and balanced way, which is reflected in the S-shaped curve of the graph.

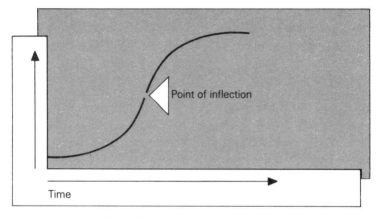

Point of inflection

Time

Sigmoid curve showing point of inflection

Qualitative change counts

The particular shape of this graph is called a Sigmoid curve, but it is the point of inflection, where the line begins to change its shape, that is crucial. It is here that something quite unexpected starts to happen that could not have been predicted from the first part of the graph. When faced with the problems of diminished food supply and overcrowding caused by the rapid changes in their environment, the yogurt bacteria overcome these problems by *changing their behaviour*. It's this change in behaviour, stepping out of the old ways of doing things, that ensures their survival. In today's world, from the techniques of intensive agriculture destroying the land, to many people's sense of dependence on low quality supermarket foods, instances abound of our own need to change our behaviour if we are going to avoid poor health, if not environmental disaster. Of course this does not mean ways we used to do things have always been wrong, it's just that they are no longer appropriate.

Before the point of inflection bacteria behave differently to those afterwards, because each group is dealing with different problems. A first stage problem is how to maximise growth. This is achieved by exponential cell division. But at the point of inflection this behaviour, if continued, would spell death to the culture when the new problem of scarcity arose. In order to survive, the bacteria change their style.

Salk suggests that if we don't want to follow the lemmings, we should take a lesson or two from a few bacteria. But how? How is it possible to initiate change in our own behaviour? According to Salk we may be at a unique point in history where the exponential change taking place all around us could undergo a qualitative shift. This is represented on the graphs of exponential change by the point of inflection. This point of inflection signals the opportunity to create a new set of values that will complete the Sigmoid curve of the graph to a successful outcome of higher level stability. Salk sees these new values as the key to creating positive change—values that can be described as the difference between an exclusive *either/or* attitude, and an inclusive *both/and* approach. What does he mean by this?

Either/or ...

Our material wealth and the incredible advance of modern technology, says Salk, have been achieved through a dualistic way of thinking summed up by the words *either/or*. Either you are my friend, or my foe. Either I win, or I lose. Either nuclear umbrella or global war. Either conservation of the environment or profit. Either homelife or career. . . . The list is endless. This attitude was useful when man was striving to control his environment, providing a safe home for his family, and satisfying his basic needs in order to survive. But now, Salk argues, it is an attitude which, if it persists, will push the growth curve into exponential doom. Instead what we need is a new *both/and* way of looking at things—one where the emphasis is on participation and co-operation. For instance: I can win *and* you can win. Both nuclear disarmament *and* peace. Ecology *and* a living. Home *and* work. . . .

Salk is suggesting that at the point of inflection there is the opportunity for us to realize we no longer have to be conditioned by the *either/or* way of looking at things, and that a more holistic approach, summarized by the words *both/and* will achieve far better results. That is certainly the vision behind *Quantum Carrot*—the future is both high-tech satellites *and* small space organic gardening, working hard *and* having fun. We don't have to choose between alternatives anymore, we can both have our cake and eat it. All that is required is to consider a new way of looking at the world. And if Salk is right, there couldn't be a more exciting time to be out on the leading edge of change than right now. In becoming aware of the changes occurring in our daily lives, instead of trying to avoid change and stick to outworn habits, we at the leading edge (the point of inflection) can make a qualitative leap in the way we think and do things.

In order to illustrate what he meant, Salk drew the graph overleaf, showing the difference between the either/or way of doing things in the past, and the both/and blueprint for the future. The future, says Salk, means man co-operating with Nature, rather than pitting himself against it. In the past, man's drive to subdue Nature through his powers of reason actually divorced him from the Earth that sustained him—an Earth which until that time he had always felt part of. Man was confronted with a choice—*either* technological advance, *or* bonding with the Earth. The possibility confronting us today is that man can have *both* his hard earned technological skill (with the material well-being that goes with it), *and* the sense of inner wealth that comes from being close to the Earth. According to Salk, a positive future lies in redressing the imbalance between man's outer ego-bound identity, and his more fundamental and inner sense of being—between his need to order and to feel connected to the Earth. This is possible through the new both/and approach to life. To look into the future without this new approach is to look nowhere.

At the global edge

Salk's concept of a shift in values to a new *both/and* way of looking at things is one of the unexpected benefits the pace of change offers us. And just as important to our aim of creating a new, health-based wealth for ourselves, is the growing awareness that for the first time in man's history, many of the most important problems facing us are at the global level. In stark contrast to life even a few decades ago, we are becoming aware that many of the issues which concern us most are not just local issues, or even national ones, but issues that affect the Earth as a whole. Perhaps as never before there is a growing sense that we are all a part of a single interrelated whole. For instance, during the Second World War, people dug for the victory of one nation over another. Now the suggestion is that people are now beginning to garden not only for themselves, or their country (though of course both are very important), but for the Earth. This holistic awareness can be illustrated by a recent survey of people who choose to buy organic food. For them the most important reason for doing so was that they felt the environment benefited through their support of organic agriculture.

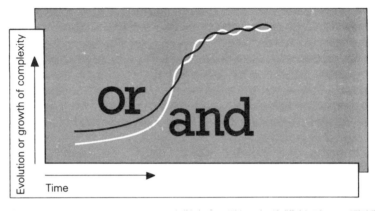

The change from an either/or position at point of inflection to a both/and approach

With the everpresent threat of nuclear oblivion, acid rain, and radioactive clouds from Chernobyl, one sometimes forgets how recent this new global awareness really is. (If you are in any doubt about this global interdependence, just check how many countries of origin make up the produce in your local shop.) Today we think nothing of picking up the phone and talking to someone thousands of miles away, or looking at weather pictures from satellites orbiting high above the Earth. And in the business world, billions of dollars, pounds, deutschmarks and yen whirl through the electronic money markets across the globe each day.

This coming together of the Earth as a whole, through the technological advances in electronics, travel and trade, as well as the growing awareness that we now have the power to destroy all life on her surface, has given us the possibility of getting back in touch with the planet—something which would never have been possible without this global awareness. It is only now, with the birth of a worldwide consciousness, that Salk's suggestion of restoring the balance between man's need to control, and his need to feel connected to the Earth, has become possible. *Quantum Carrot* suggests that the sense of well-being which comes from feeling connected to our Earth—a sense which many of us lose from time to time in the bustle of modern life—is now available to us again through the techniques of small space organic gardening, without having to give up the benefits of our post-industrial society. To regain that sense of life's depth, we no longer have to 'opt out' into a life of self-sufficiency. With the new sense of living in a global community, we can see that in the act of producing delicious organic vegetables for ourselves, even if only in a window box on the kitchen window sill, we are working to heal the Earth in ways as diverse as increasing the life of her soils that help maintain the planet's life support systems, to our own changed attitude that now seeks to work with the Earth rather than exploit her.

Wealth creates more wealth

Symbolizing the new global level we find ourselves operating on are the pictures of the Earth brought back by the Apollo astronauts: '*It was a beautiful, harmonious, peaceful-looking planet, blue with white clouds, and one that gave you a deep sense . . . of home, of being, of identity. It is what I prefer to call instant global consciousness*', wrote Edgar Mitchell when he returned from the Apollo XII mission. Peter Russell, in his book *The Awakening Earth*, comments: '*The most valuable spin-off from moon expeditions may not have been in the fields of science, economics, politics, or the military, but in the field of consciousness*'.

Like all symbols, the pictures of our planet pulsing with life in the blackness of space give valuable clues to the process it represents. For instance, it is a picture of unity and harmony, of the interconnection of things. It came from the most technically advanced project undertaken by man, yet the picture has the simplicity of a child's drawing. Only technical hardware made it possible, yet it portrays a living, organic unity. And despite the chaos which now surrounds us, the symbol speaks of tranquility and well-being. The suggestion of *Quantum Carrot* is that these are the rewards of the new ecological wealth of the 80's, the way to which is summed up in the words '*Think Globally, Act Locally*'. This wealth is available to all of us as long as we do not shy away from our fast changing world, but choose to see the problems facing us as opportunities for finding new richness in our lives. How these new riches differ from the material affluence that no longer provides lasting satisfaction is the question we must turn to now.

TWO

The Riches of the 80's

Have you ever noticed that in the old Hollywood films the first thing the rich and famous do when they enter a room is to fix themselves a drink? And after that they probably light up a cigarette, the implication being that if you are rich and famous you drink and smoke. Advertisements are full of similar implications—that drinking a certain kind of rum or vermouth will bring you a taste of the exciting jet-set life while cigarette smoking is toted as the ultimate in urbane sophistication.

Strange as it may sound, the assumptions behind these advertisement campaigns appear out of line with a shift that's taking place in what people really value. In striking defiance to the 'success images' we are sold in many advertisements, we in the Western world are becoming increasingly concerned with health. A recent Gallup poll showed that, unlike twenty years ago, today's success symbols tend to be the things money *can't* buy, such as a happy family, an enjoyable job, and most of all (the top success goal mentioned by 58% of the people surveyed) *good health*.

Health has become a fascination with most people—but it is no longer information about the latest heart transplant technique or miracle drug which people are craving. Their interest is increasingly centred around what they can do for themselves to improve the quality of their lives, their vitality, their emotional and physical health. Using the techniques of small space organic gardening is one way to maximize this well-being with the best natural source of high level nutrition available anywhere—freshly harvested organic vegetables. But health is just the cornerstone of this shift in values in the Western world. The techniques of *Quantum Carrot* can create a greater sense of well-being than by just providing high quality food.

The new values

According to Daniel Yankelovich, a leading American researcher into changing values, this value shift has brought with it '*an outburst of sheer vitality and ingenuity and ability to cope . . . a profound change in the concerns that drive our society and our politics and shape our economy'.* The new values of the 80's are centred on a person's desire for self expression—the wish to discover their full potential, grounded in such down-to-earth realities as their bodies. *'You feel a zest for the game of living and being for its own sake'*, says Yankelovich. Aerobic classes, additive-free food and interest in organic produce are just a few indicators of this new concern with health, physical well-being and energy levels which are essential if we are to realize fully our capabilities.

A few years ago the new wealth we are after would have been impossible. At that time we were still bound up with old exploitive forms of behaviour which were mirrored back to us by the way we stripped the Earth of her resources. Until we became aware of this dangerous behaviour towards our environment we would have been unable to treat ourselves in any other but exploitive ways. At first sight this may sound suprising, but there are still many signs of this exploitive approach to ourselves, not least the 'Volkswagon consciousness' where many people run themselves as long and hard as they can and expect their doctors to replace the worn out parts. One young businessman I know gets his best kicks from working like a dog all day then going out at night, returning home drunk at five in the morning to catch a couple of hours sleep before the next day's work. We still continue in these old habit patterns, but perhaps for the first time we are becoming aware of the possibility we can change.

Perhaps more than any other factor, the growing awareness of the harm we have done to the Earth has moved our hearts to look for a new way of being that does not need to exploit or dominate, and part of our new wealth is beginning to turn this new sense of compassion for living things towards ourselves. It is this ability of our actions towards the Earth to mirror the way we think and feel about ourselves that is one of the reasons why Gaia (the ancient Greek name for the Earth) is intricately bound up in the new wealth of the 80's we wish to create. And that in turn is another way small space organic gardening can help create that wealth beyond just producing delicious high level nourishment—the way we garden can be like a microcosm of how we generally treat ourselves and our approach to the Earth as a whole. Even so, there are still a few more unexpected qualities surrounding this new wealth.

Everybody gets rich

Perhaps one of the most striking qualities of the 80's desire for health, well-being and the realization of personal potential (a quality which sets it apart from the material affluence of previous decades) is that the new wealth of one person increases the wealth of us all. Unlike the struggle for material wealth that dominated our society in the post-war industrial boom in which one person's wealth was often had at the expense of another's, the new wealth that we are interested in here is *increased* by more people participating in it. How can this be possible?

Material wealth of earlier decades was largely based on the sense that one got rich at the expense of someone or something else, either through the use of other people's labour, or by processing one of the Earth's natural resources. In either case, the principle was one of exploitation where one was either a winner or a loser. Usually it was the Earth that was the loser. In direct contrast to this, the new wealth is based on co-operation. If we support organic farmers by purchasing organic produce, we all gain from diminished use of pesticides, through less chance of 'spraydrift' exposure, the return of wildlife to the hedgerows, and the opportunity for our soils to recover their natural vitality so that they can grow high quality food again. The more people that support organic agriculture, or start to grow their own organic food anywhere in the world, the more each of us gains through the security of a stable ecosystem, trade with countries free from war and strife (which comes from a scarcity of resources), and the pleasure in feeling part of a community with such power for positive change.

With the new wealth based on a sense of co-operation, personal power and autonomy there are no losers because by doing the best for yourself you are also doing the best for the environment and the Earth. You know how you can raise the energy in a room if you feel good yourself. Other people, even if they were low in spirits, will start to smile and laugh because feeling good is contagious, it's a wealth made to be shared—a wealth which it doesn't make sense to hoard. The wealth of the 80's is a win/win situation—the wealth of one person can contribute to the wealth of all. This win/win situation is part of the changing values that Jonas Salk suggested could mark the transition from a period of exponential change to a new, higher order level of stability. How does this relate to small space organic gardening?

Creating organic wealth

Remember how vegetables used to taste? And when baked potatoes did not shrivel to nothing? With the *Quantum Carrot* approach to small space gardening this new concept of wealth is not an ideal for the future, it's available right now, whether you live in a stately mansion or town flat. With the Absolute Beginners chapter (see p. 76 for details) you can begin to feel the good effects of your work almost immediately. The high vitality organic foods you produce, combined, for instance, with a high raw food diet plan like the one outlined in Leslie and Susannah Kenton's book *Raw Energy*, will have you looking forward to getting up in the mornings, full of energy for the whole day. With the burden of unwanted pesticide residues eased, your body can begin to return to its natural sense of well-being. And all this wealth creation can be had far cheaper than lower quality supermarket foods.

The rich patterns of green in your garden or window box are new status symbols of your wealth. Your indoor plants can bring Gaia's organic splendour into your own home. Just imagine the sweet Mediterranean scent of rosemary in the hallway, or a hanging basket of mint and strawberries to add fragrance and colour to some corner of the room.

I have also found my garden has also brought me many like-minded friends who are always dropping by to give advice on carrot varieties, and swap notes on root fly problems. Without their generosity I would have never been able to start growing, ignorant as I was of the simplest gardening methods. There is nothing quite like leaning over the fence and discussing the latest techniques of slug control! But perhaps my greatest sense of well-being comes as I work in the garden, turning the compost, or trimming the herbs, and I become aware of an immense sense of purpose in what I am doing, the pleasure that comes from feeling what I do is important both for myself and also now for the Earth—a sense of meaning that is often lacking in many jobs today. This sense of meaning and the pleasure it brings is not just my own individual experience, it seems always a part of this new wealth that the 80's people, in their own ways, are starting to create all over the world.

The nouveaux riches

Where in the world are peoples standing up and demanding to be rich? Almost everywhere you look. In the Himalayas the Chipko movement has been organized by the local communities and is spreading across the area. Village women stream out of their villages when they see commercial loggers approach and hug the trees, protecting their riches with their own bodies. These riches fill their lives with beauty, protect their soil from erosion, maintain a continuous clean water supply, and fill the air with the sheltered micro-climate only forest can create. Such wealth cannot be found in affluent downtown New York or London, and is sadly missing from the most of our lives, whether we live in a developed country or in the Third World.

But you will find it in Soweto where amazing Graze Sesali, a nurse and mother of four, has organized the youths of her town to clean up the 'stinking hell-hole' of her rubbish strewn street. In its place they planted trees, grass, created boundaries and gave the parks names. That was October 1985. Today you can't walk far without seeing these colourful parks, each with its own identity—Villa Park, The Park with a Mind of its Own, Freedom Park. Benches, play areas and the boundaries have been made from various scraps which Soweto is littered. Money is collected from local residents and passing cars to pay for paint, more trees and compost. Neighbours willingly allow the young people to use their water for the plants. If you stop to look around the parks, you will immediately be greeted by a proud and enthusiastic group of young people who jealously protect their parks from refuse and carelessness, with signs reading 'Welcome to cool'n tidy park, we love you' and 'Don't litter everywhere'.

You will also find it in the Berkshire home of the famous Nature-cure doctors Gordon and Barbara Latto, who for years have lived in unmitigated splendour centred around their modest garden which they have transformed into an Earthly paradise, keeping bees, growing all their fresh food organically, filling their house and clinic with flowers year round, and participating in all this beauty despite starting work at five in the morning and finishing past ten at night. Indeed they can only work so hard because they are so rich. It's their garden that nourishes them and sustains them so they can help their patients. All this wealth comes from a new relationship with the Earth. With *Quantum Carrot* this wealth is available through small space organic gardening. But how does the Earth create such splendour? What goes on in her soil that man, despite all his ingenuity, cannot begin to imitate? It is that world which we turn to now.

THREE

What is Organic Gardening?

'*Without the soil the farmer is nothing. But if he feels, hears and understands its message, then there is nothing he cannot do.*'

SIR ALBERT HOWARD

When I talk to other people about organic gardening it is usually against the background of the chemical nightmare that annually pours 5 billion gallons of pesticides on our food and contributes to the erosion of the 12 million acres of land made agriculturally worthless each year through poor land management. Set against this, the world of organic growing could not be more different. In many ways this contrast reflects the present shift in values we have noticed between a now dangerously inappropriate way of being based on the exploitation of resources and the desire to create a new sense of wealth through close co-operation with the environment. Like the two halves of Jonas Salk's sigmoid curve, divided by the point of inflection, conventional agriculture is an instance of the either/or way of thinking where wealth can be gained only at the expense of something else, while the organic agricultural systems of the 80's have as their starting point man's close relationship with a living soil that he feeds and sustains so that, in turn, it can feed his crops both now and far into the distant future.

One popular misconception about organic growing is that it is nothing but a denial of modern technology and the return to the past where men scratched a living from the Earth with just an ox and wooden plough. It is certainly true that organic growing takes the best from the past, but far from being stuck there, today's organic systems are fast becoming potent and effective growing systems—for conventional and organic growers alike. New biological controls introduced into commercial greenhouse tomato and cucumber production (where even the most powerful pesticides had failed) is just one example. Instead of being a return to the past, all the signs are that organic growing will be one of the leading 'soft' technologies of the future.

The principles of organic gardening

But for all its importance in our fast changing world, the principles behind organic growing are remarkably simple. First of all there is nothing more important to an organic grower, whether farmer or gardener, than the *soil*. Unlike the soluble mineral fertilizers and sprays of the conventional grower, the soil is the powerhouse of the organic garden. And rather than an inert medium for plants while they grow, it is a living world that creates crops of the highest quality. Organic systems feed the soil, and then let the soil feed the plants.

The second principle of organic growing is that the organic grower thinks in terms of cycles instead of production lines. In order to make sure our land will continue producing bountiful crops, as far as possible organic growers return to the land what they have taken out by composting all organic wastes. And if that isn't enough, they beg, steal, or buy in more organic matter, although this is always secondary to producing their own fertility.

And the final principle of organic systems is their approach to health. Unlike our conventional counterparts, we rarely have nightmares over pests and diseases. Organic growers recognize that Nature takes no special precautions over these—every forest is full of pests and disease of every kind, but they are kept in balance by the whole web of life. It's the health of the soil that deals with 90% of our pest problems. Without this health the chemical grower is forced to use sprays because, like a sickly child, his plants lack the vitality to help themselves. As Dr Albrecht, agronomist at the University of Missouri puts it: '*Insects and disease are the symptoms of a failing crop, not the cause*'. So what is the power in the soil that can keep even the most devastating pests at bay?

The gregarious, dynamic, completely unintelligible soil

Quite simply, it is life itself. If you thought you were going to garden alone, then you will have to think again. In every teaspoon of fertile soil there are 4 billion microscopic bacteria whose life cycles interweave with the countless protozoa, fungi, ants, wireworms, termites, snails, grasshoppers, worms, earwigs, and many more creatures that form the web of soil life that is the basis of plant vitality. What is going on in your garden makes the patterns and interconnections of the world's largest computers look like free gifts from the cereal packet. In fact, what many people think of as simply mud or dirt, is an infinitely complex piece of biological engineering. And like all highly evolved organisms, the soil has basic needs of survival in the form of food, air, water, and warmth, if it is going to work for you. In order to understand how the soil meets these basic needs we need to understand how it is built.

Soil structure

In a good garden soil, just under half consists of mineral particles that have been formed over the centuries by the breakdown of rock. The size of these particles determines your soil type. Large particles, about 1mm (⅛in) across, are called sand. A single sand particle could be broken down into 1,000,000 silt particles, and each of these could weigh as much as 1,000 particles of clay.

Most soils are a combination of these and according to the balance in them are called clays, loams, or sands. Each will have its own qualities. For example, a clay will hold water well, making it useful in drought conditions, but it is slow to warm up at the beginning of the season because air cannot circulate freely. Sand warms well, is light and easy to work with, but has difficulty holding nutrients or water which run away quickly through the large gaps between the particles. A loam is somewhere between the two.

People say an ideal soil is a 'medium loam' as it possesses the advantages but none of the extremes of clay or sand, and would be a mixture of different particle sizes. However, it's not so much particle size that determines the strength of your soil, as the all important 3–10% organic matter that has the essential function of maintaining soil structure and release of nutrients to plants. This witch's cauldron of animal and vegetable remains, compost, humus and billions of micro-organisms binds the mineral particles into soil crumbs. If you pick up a handful of soil and push it through your fingers, you can break it down so far, but after that only the crumbs are left, and they are what give the soil its structure. It is the loss of this essential soil structure through modern chemical agriculture that is causing the United States to lose well over a billion tonnes of topsoil a year and threatens long-term food production.

Soil crumbs or granules give stability to a soil. In heavy clays, they open out the structure that prevents waterlogging. As the water drains away, air can circulate, warming the soil and letting the micro-organisms breathe. In sandy soils the crumbs bind the reluctant sand particles together, helping them retain water and nutrients, and protecting them from wind and water erosion.

Good structure through soil crumbs goes a long way towards providing air, water and warmth to the living organisms—three of the four basic needs of the soil. The fourth need is food. How can we feed the soil so that the soil in turn can feed our plants?

Kitchen waste is food for your soil

Suprisingly the organic material we normally throw away is the nourishment a healthy soil needs. Old carrot tops, tea leaves, and banana skins come high up on the menu, but any properly composted organic material gives the soil life. That includes: kitchen waste, newspapers, animal manures, the dead bodies of soil organisms such as soil bacteria, fungi and worms, straw, grass cuttings. . . . Organic waste is the fuel of the soil, completing Nature's cycle by putting back into the land what has been taken out through plant and animal growth. The great British champion of organic gardening, Sir Albert Howard, describes this process as the 'Wheel of Life', the never-ending cycle of birth, growth, maturity, death and decay—'*The revolutions of this Wheel never falter and are perfect. Death supersedes life and life rises again from what is dead and decayed*'.

This law of return is the crux of organic gardening. The British Organic Standards Committee states: '*The development of biological cycles involving micro-organisms, soil fauna, plants and animals is the basis of organic agriculture*'. Soil life benefits from the law of return not only because organic matter provides the basis for essential soil structure that cannot be sustained through any other means, but is also a source of food for soil organisms—quite literally, the soil eats your rubbish. Properly fed, the soil can now get down to feeding you through the controlled release of plant nutrients essential for healthy growth.

What makes plants grow?

Early in the nineteenth century a renowned German chemist, Justis von Liebig, in a brilliant series of experiments, analysed the ashes of burnt plants and identified the three major elements needed for plant growth: nitrogen (N), phosphorus (P_2O_5) and potash (K_2O), commonly called N, P and K. Chemical growers, with their reductionist approach, took Liebig's conclusions to mean that these three elements were *all* plants needed for growth and that they could be supplied through chemical means. The chemical fertilizer we know today consists of soluble mineral salts, factory-produced from oil and scarce mineral reserves around the world, synthesized in a proportion of N, P and K according to the specific needs of the grower. But Nature would not have created a bio-technology as intricate as the soil just to provide three basic nutrients to plants. The simplistic approach of chemical agriculture now produces plants deficient in essential trace elements—deficiencies that are passed on to us in the food we eat. In Japan 60% of intensive grassland has been shown to be deficient in potassium, 30% in zinc, 50% in boron, and 25% in molybdenum— even though we now realize that apart from N, P and K, plants also need traces of boron, calcium, chlorine, copper, fluorine, magnesium, manganese, molybdenum, nickle, silicon and zinc and a whole host of other elements whose role in plant life we have not yet begun to understand.

Chemical companies finally caught on that trace elements were needed for healthy growth and started adding minute quantities out of their chemist's bag to the NPK. But instead of solving problems, these manufactured trace elements have presented us and the soil with new dangers—many of the elements never break down in the soil, and yearly additions finally create toxic conditions where the soil can no longer support life. This is because trace elements are quite literally traces. For instance 0.01 parts per million of boron can cause deficiency symptoms in some plants, while 1.0 p.p.m. is toxic to other plants. Healthy organic soils can carefully regulate these levels while chemically degraded soils cannot—an excellent example of how the new organic way of doing things can have far more success than the old redundant chemical approach to food production. But not only are the sources of plant food different in conventional and organic systems, the pathways that get that food into the plant also show how conventional and organic agriculture are based on two entirely different ways of looking at the world—one based on a mechanical view of the universe derived from the 19th century physics of Sir Isaac Newton, and the other mirroring the 20th century findings at the quantum physical levels of reality. It is through the little understood interaction between plant and organic soil life (which mirror some events at these levels), that we are able to create delicious, organic vegetables high in nutritional quality.

How does the soil feed my plants?

Plants grown under either chemical or organic conditions will both take up nutrients in soluble form through the transpiration process where water is pulled into the plant from the soil and given off through the leaves. But whereas this is the only way plants can take up nutrients without the life of the soil, organic vegetables rely on an 'active' feeding process between their roots and soil organisms. For instance, along every root are millions of microscopic root hairs— transparent and living only a few days. Lawrence Hills, director of the Henry Doubleday Research Association, explains that as they die these root hairs release proteins and carbohydrates on which friendly bacteria feed, which, through the process of feeding, also make plant food minerals available for absorption by living rootlets. These in turn aid the breakdown process by secreting digestive juices that further dissolve the root hairs. As this process continues it is very difficult to distinguish what is soil and what is root, as the two are continually interchanged in the dynamic process of root hair formation, digestion, absorption and renewal.

In a similar way, early researchers into quantum physics found that as they approached the smallest levels of reality (smaller even than the parts of an atom), they found it was no longer obvious what they were looking at. For instance, according to the way they chose to set up the experiment, they could be either mapping a wave field or tracking a particle. This forced them to suggest that instead of the world being built out of separate 'building blocks' like atoms, at its roots reality looked more like an integrated, indivisible whole, and it was us, through our approach to that reality, that split this whole into separate parts. The wholeness they discovered we now find reflected in the dynamic interaction of plant and the living soil of organic husbandry.

Perhaps this interpenetrating wholeness that forms the basis of organic plant nutrition is most vividly illustrated by the fascinating mycorrhizal fungi. These soil organisms live with one half of their glistening white threads weaving through the soil, the other half probing deep into the root cells. Experiments have shown fungal threads actively moving towards young roots, entering the cell walls, and passing from cell to cell where, in return for carbohydrate energy foods, they contribute moisture, nitrogen, and other nutrients to the plant which finally absorbs them into its own tissues. The fungal threads are very rich in protein, and may contain as much as 10%

organic nitrogen for the plant to use in growth. It is living connections like these that create strong, healthy abundance in the organic garden. Nevertheless, whatever the fascination these microscopic dynamics may have for us, no account of organic gardening would be complete without a tribute to the 'king of the soil', the mighty worm.

The mighty worm

Pride of place in the organic garden goes to the worm because of the work he does to create organic splendour. Results from Lunt and Jacobson at Connecticut Experiment Station show earthworm casts are five times richer in combined nitrogen, seven times richer in available phosphate, and eleven times richer in potash than the upper 15cm (6in) of soil. It is estimated that up to four million worms deposit twenty-five tons/tonnes of this elixir on every acre of fertile land each year. And not only are these casts 40% richer in soil building humus than surface soil, containing three times more calcium and available magnesium, but their bodies when they die can produce up to 45kg (100lbs) of nitrogen fertilizer per acre (0.4 hectare) per year.

With credentials like these it is easy to see why the worm is the organic gardener's best friend. But it is not just nutrients that he can provide. The worm pre-dated the plough and continues to outperform it at every turn. Relentlessly the earthworm breaks up the soil, digs tunnels that improve aeration and water flow, and increases the humus content by eating organic waste. As well as this, he actively builds soil crumbs, essential for soil structure, by ingesting soil and fresh organic residues. Using organic stabilizing gums and lime secreted from a special gland in the digestive tract, the worm is able to cement soil particles together.

Chemical growing cannot reap the same rewards from these creatures, praised by Charles Darwin as being able to '*prepare the ground in excellent manner*'. Chemical fertilizers often create an excess of nitrogen that turns to acid in the soil. This acid is intolerable to the worm. In Australia the nine feet (2.7m) long earthworms have become extinct through Superphosphate ferttilizer application. Even if soil conditions are not too acid or filled with pesticide residue, low humus starves the worms away from inhospitable land into richer, organic pasture. Professor Hardy Voltmann of Kassel University, West Germany, tells of entire fields of worms migrating from a conventional farm to its organic neighbour.

The secret of keeping your worms happy is to feed them plenty of organic matter. And the methods of *Gaiaculture* help create the right conditions to keep your worms exactly where they can do the best for you, because as we have seen in this chapter, maximizing the life of your soil is the best way to reap the richest harvest. However, those harvests do not just mean a beautiful garden and delicious vegetables for ourselves, they are also a start to renewing the vitality of the Earth as a whole, which we have seen is as much bound up in the new wealth we seek as a good supply of fresh organic produce. And if it was a surprise to find such an abundance of life in the ground beneath your feet, one of the most novel suggestions put forward by a scientist in recent years is Jim Lovelock's hypothesis that the Earth we live on may be a living organism itself.

FOUR

The Gaia Hypothesis

Unexpected friends turn up when we begin to discard old world-views and forms of behaviour, like the billions of soil organisms jealously nurturing our organic crops and bringing the pulse of life to the soil. Still, who would have imagined that our greatest ally, in our bid to create a new wealth, may be the planet we inhabit? Like a living organism, she maintains the precise conditions on her surface we need in order to survive. This is the hypothesis put forward by Jim Lovelock, an independent scientist who has co-operated with NASA on their space exploration programme, and is now visiting professor in the Department of Cybernetics at Reading University, England. Perhaps more than any other single idea, Lovelock's hypothesis—which he has named 'Gaia', the ancient Greek name for Mother Earth—shows the opportunities for positive change that come from the radical new ways of looking at ourselves and the world we live in. The Gaia hypothesis is nothing short of a revolution in thought that is gaining wide approval from leading scientists as they find its suggestions help solve nagging problems in their own fields.

Before the Gaia hypothesis, old ways of looking at the Earth were bound up with the world-view of Newtonian physics. Based on Newton's mechanical models, the Earth was just another planet in the solar system, admittedly one with an unique thin crust of biological life, but still subject to the same laws of gravity and motion as other planets. Without the sense of organic unity created by Lovelock's suggestions, the Newtonian world-view saw the Earth's natural resources as little more than raw materials for our industries. To farmers, politicians, or businessmen who remain trapped in the Newtonian way of looking at things, wealth is still generated through the exploitation of these fast diminishing natural resources. It is dangerous old habit patterns like these, warns Lovelock, that may have brought us to the end of life on Earth. The muds we dredge from the oceans and the forests we cut down are not just the raw materials for new products, they are the living body of Gaia. If old habits, which do not recognize Gaia's biological life support systems, continue, these systems will weaken, fail, and all life will cease. But if this does not seem the best way of making use of the opportunities before us, let's look at just how Lovelock discovered Gaia, and through what processes she works.

The discovery of Gaia

The Gaia hypothesis grew out of Lovelock's involvement with NASA during the late 1960's. Together with other scientists, Lovelock was busy finding ways of detecting life on the other planets, especially Mars. The problem with most of the experiments suggested was that they were based on the assumption that life on Mars would be similar to life on Earth.

But what if life on Mars was totally different to this carbon- and water-based life we know so well? Lovelock started looking at ways of detecting *any* life forms, whatever their chemical makeup. The first thing he noticed was that all living organisms interact with their environment. From the simplest cell to the largest dinosaur, all organisms gather food from their surroundings, and excrete waste products as an intricate part of their life metabolism. This meant, thought Lovelock, that an environment containing life would be constantly changing as a result of that life and an environment without life would tend towards a state of chemical equilibrium.

From these observations Lovelock suggested to his colleagues at NASA that planets whose environment was close to chemical equilibrium would be unlikely to have life. But if the environment was different from the chemist's predictions, then that would be a strong indicator of life's presence.

Using the results from infra-red astronomy, Lovelock compared the atmospheric compositions of Mars and Venus with that of Earth. They showed the atmosphere of Mars and Venus close to the predicted chemical equilibrium expected of a lifeless planet. So far the Voyager space probes have confirmed Lovelock's prediction that there is no life on Mars.

But what of the Earth? '*In the infra-red the Earth radiates its signature of life so clearly as to be recognisable from well outside the solar system*', writes Lovelock. Compared to a planet without life, the Earth's atmosphere displays all the signs of profound change through life forms that cover her surface. Still more intriguing is that *the*

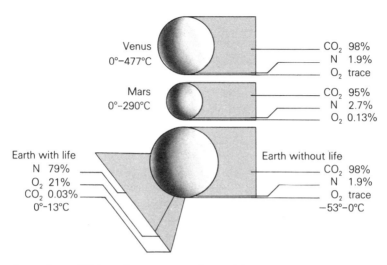

Venus
0°–477°C
CO_2 98%
N 1.9%
O_2 trace

Mars
0°–290°C
CO_2 95%
N 2.7%
O_2 0.13%

Earth with life
N 79%
O_2 21%
CO_2 0.03%
0°–13°C

Earth without life
CO_2 98%
N 1.9%
O_2 trace
−53°–0°C

Atmosphere of lifeless planets compared to earth's atmosphere

atmospheric composition of the Earth is superbly adapted to sustain life. What's more, it has been this way for hundreds of millions of years. It's this remarkable life support system that led Lovelock to Gaia.

Who is maintaining our life support systems?

Over the last three and a half billion years life has evolved on this planet, the Earth's average temperature has been maintained within the narrow bounds of 10–20°C (50–68°F), ideal conditions for life. This could possibly be explained by some fluke, or fortuitous combination of gases and distance from the sun, until we realize that during that same time the sun's output has increased by at least 30%. Research by Yugoslav meteororologist Mihalanovich has shown that the last few ice ages are the result of minute changes of the Earth's orbit around the sun. A mere 2% decrease in the temperature of one hemisphere is enough to bring on the next ice age. Just imagine then what a 30% increase would do! But if living matter is not passive to threats to its existence such as the increased heat from the sun, what are the active mechanisms involved?

With no explanation available for our understanding of the Earth and its processes based on the traditional Newtonian world-view, Lovelock was finally forced to go beyond these norms and look at the possibility that life itself regulated its own environment on a global scale through an intricate system of biological feedback mechanisms similar to the way we regulate temperature and other functions in our own bodies. How do these feedback mechanisms work?

The organs of our bodies from the brain to endocrine glands are very sensitive to changes in temperature, so that even a few degrees either side of 37°C (98.6°F) can mean death. In order to maintain this homeostasis (a word from Greek which means 'to stay the same'), the body has developed feedback mechanisms which monitor any slight changes in the body temperature and 'feed' the information back to the central nervous system which initiates a response to compensate for the change. For instance, if our body sensors report that our body temperature is beginning to fall, we may start shivering—one way the body creates heat is through muscle activity. When our temperature returns to normal, the sensors stop sending signals to our brain, which in turn stops sending its heat-generating commands.

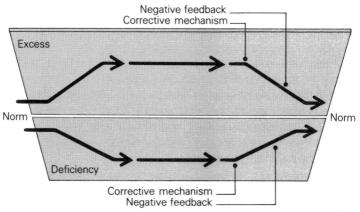

Negative feedback loop

Faced with evidence of precise control of all life-support functions on Earth for the last 4 billion years, Lovelock had to look at the possibility, however improbable it seemed at the time, that the Earth contained biofeedback mechanisms as complex as those within us, through which she maintained the right conditions for life. But it was not just temperature control that kept Gaia at work. There were other signs that the Earth behaved like a living organism.

Biofeedback mechanisms at work

Lovelock's investigations highlighted just how fragile the conditions are for life on Earth, life which could not have been maintained uninterrupted for thousands of millions of years without some active global biofeedback mechanism. For instance;

★ The salt content of the oceans has remained a constant 3.4% for aeons, despite new deposits being continually washed down from the mountains. If the salt concentration had ever changed, even for just a few moments, to above 6%, all aquatic life would literally have been 'blown apart' through osmotic pressure bursting cell walls.

★ The oxygen content of the atmosphere remains at 21% with good reason; a few percent less and we could not produce enough energy to survive, a few percent more and even damp vegetation would burn well. Forest fires could sweep across the planet, and destroy all vegetation.

★ There is just enough ammonia in the atmosphere to neutralize naturally produced sulphuric and nitric acids. This keeps rainfall at a pH tolerable to plants and animals.

★ The ozone layer in the upper atmosphere shields us from ultra-violet radiation that can damage essential molecules for life, including DNA with its genetic coding.

Lovelock's Gaia hypothesis suggests that there is no other way for these conditions of life to have been maintained for so long except through complex biofeedback mechanisms similar to those that operate in living organisms, including our own bodies. With these biofeedback mechanisms the Earth seems to function like a living organism, and it is this global process that Lovelock called Gaia. But his hardest task still lay in explaining just how Gaia kept such perfect global homeostasis.

The surprising answer was that Gaia's biofeedback mechanisms seem to rely on *biological life itself*. Gaia maintains life support systems by co-ordinating the billions of organisms in the soil, marshes, and oceans, together with the millions of plant species across her surface. For instance, Lovelock suggests that if global temperature begins to increase, biofeedback loops increase evaporation of the oceans and transpiration in the rainforests. This global 'sweating' process not only cools the Earth, but creates huge blankets of white cloud that reflect the sun's rays back into space. In this way Gaia co-ordinates living organisms to maintain planetary life support systems. Another example may be the methane produced through the fermentation process of countless bacteria in swamps and mudflats all over the world. This, proposes Lovelock, could regulate excess oxygen by combining with it, taking 2,000 tons/tonnes of oxygen out of the atmosphere each year.

Taken as a whole, the evidence of global feedback mechanisms and the crucial role of the planet's ecology in maintaining them confronts us with possibility that we are living on a creature so large that we are like specks of sand on her surface, and so regulated that she has maintained essential conditions for life over thousands of millions of years. While some people are still trapped into thinking of the Earth as just another planet, where, either by some freak of chance, or cosmic joke, we live on out in a far flung corner of the galaxy, others are beginning to wonder at the possibilities available if we start to align ourselves with Gaia's life-giving power.

The power of Gaia

Faced as we are by a crisis brought about by the fast accelerating pace of change and aggravated by die-hard habits, perhaps Gaia's greatest strength at the moment lies in her ability to wake us up to the real nature of this crisis. One way this may be happening is for Gaia to act as a mirror to ourselves, reflecting back the image we cast across her surface. For instance, while according to Harvard's professor Edward O. Wilson, there is far more biological complexity in a handful of Virginia soil than on the entire surface of Jupiter, we destroy this biological treasure house at a rate of 4 tonnes/tons per ½ hectare/1 acre per year in the United States through modern intensive agriculture. Famine- and war-torn Ethiopia, just one sixth the size of the United States, is reputed to be losing the same amount of topsoil each year. Facts like these may come just in time for us to see just what it is within us that is creating a desert out of our planet. But rather than some evil darkness of human nature, I am inclined to believe many of the problems we have created, from denatured food to excessive environmental pollution, are the result of an old, outmoded world-view that simply has not changed with the times.

Gaia mirrors back to us the poverty we create if we don't free ourselves from a mechanistic view of the universe that treats the Earth as a resource to be exploited, and leaves us feeling powerless to make the positive changes we want in our own lifestyles. But far from this being just a story of gloom and doom, the very acknowledgement of the Earth as a living creature has begun a new tale of how we are able to turn the crisis that now faces us into a new source of ecological wealth.

Gaia and man walk into the unknown

Gaia is not only a mirror to ourselves, she also displays the power of living organisms on a grand scale. In a constantly changing solar system, she has created a living abundance, to our knowledge, unparalleled anywhere in the galaxy. As life has evolved, Gaia has found novel ways to regulate the new oxygen created by plants, the salt content of the oceans, and even the felling of temperate forests during the last 8,000 years as man began to clear Gaia's surface for agricultural purposes.

Until now, Gaia has turned any new problems into opportunities to further her rich biological systems that are her flesh and blood. If at any stage Gaia had baulked at change, that wealth would have quickly vanished, leaving her like Venus—dead.

But despite her power, Gaia has never experienced a time of such rapid change over the past 3.5 billion years as she has this century. What's more, these changes have been brought about by part of herself that has 'come of age' in the sense that this organism now has the power consciously to disrupt Gaia's feedback mechanisms to such an extent that they may break down. This organism is man. Maybe the reason Gaia is putting so much effort into mirroring back an image of ourselves is that we are now the decisive factor as to whether life continues on the planet.

In *The Awakening Earth*, global consultant Peter Russell goes as far as to suggest that human beings may now play an important role in Gaia's nervous system, gathering information about her processes through satellite pictures and scientific journals, and giving early warning of any imminent danger. Acting as a mirror to our behaviour, Gaia may be asking us not only to provide warning of ecological danger, but also to understand the nature of the problem and implement a solution. And of all the ecological danger sites of the world, none has been the focus of so much attention as the clearing of the Amazon rainforests. Why is this?

The Polonoroeste Project

Gaia's rainforests, a larger part of them in the Amazon basin, not only contain half her total genetic diversity, but, according to Lovelock, may also play a crucial role in regulating temperature, carbon dioxide and oxygen levels, the cycling of nutrients through the atmosphere, and global weather patterns. Warning sirens blast from this area of the globe because at the moment we are cutting tropical forest down at a rate of 100 acres a minute, a good chunk of this in the Amazon basin. In Brazil, this is the declared ambition of the Northwest Development (Polonoroeste) programme. The World Bank, with its aim to fund world development, has put $443 million of the $1.6 billion cost of the project. The main part of the loan is for a central highway and the rest is for feeder roads. The role of the highway, which cuts through the heart of the southwestern Amazon basin, is to attract thousands of settlers to an area of Amazon forest three quarters the size of France. If the present trends continue, the entire Brazilian state of Rondonia, an area the size of Great Britain, will be deforested by 1990.

What will be the outcome of this destruction? Lovelock, at a recent conference in Brazil, told delegates that we cannot predict the consequences of changes on this scale. *'It is a question like asking: What is the proportion of the skin area that can be burnt without suffering significant systems failure. We do not yet know whether the tropical forest systems are vital to the present planet ecology'*, he told the conference. The destruction of the Brazilian rainforest is bringing us face to face with an uncertain future. The one thing that is certain is that the rainforests challenge us to begin our new roles as global guardians, for the sake of continued life on Earth, and for the new 80's wealth we want for ourselves. But this means more than just raising the alarm. What are the causes behind the danger, and what cure can we bring? These are the questions that face us now.

What is really going on in the Amazon basin?

On 19 September 1984, the esteemed Brazilian agronomist, José Lutzenberger, gave his testimony before the Subcommittee on Natural Resources, Agriculture Research and Environment of the House Committee on Science and Technology in Washington. In it he showed the deforestation of Rondonia in the Polonoroeste Project cannot, as is generally assumed, be attributed to the need for more land to feed the growing population.

To begin with, the soils under the tropical rainforest are the poorest in the world. Permanently high temperatures and high rainfall leech away all the mineral nutrients. Perhaps as much as 90% of tropical moist forest soils are completely unsuited for any kind of permanent annual agriculture. The only people that have evolved sustainable agro-ecosystems in these areas are the indigenous tribal peoples that inhabit many of the still intact rainforests. This may explain why a survey conducted by USAID in 1980 of six settlement projects in the Peruvian Amazon revealed settler desertion and abandonment rates ranging from 26–92%; three of the six projects had been virtually abandoned by their intended 'beneficiaries'. Guppy, a recent visitor to these areas of 'development', wrote in the journal *Foreign Affairs*: '*Visiting such areas it is hard to view without emotion the miles of devastated trees, of felled, broken and burned trunks, of branches, mud, and bark crisscrossed with tractor trails—especially when one realizes that in most cases nothing of comparable value will grow again in the area. Such sights are reminiscent of photographs of Hiroshima, and Brazil and Indonesia might be regarded as waging the equivalent of thermo-nuclear war upon their territories*'. Does this bear any signs of a project that is going to create any kind of wealth for anyone? And if not, what has caused such a disaster?

From his in-depth analysis of the facts, Lutzenberger concludes that the World Bank is funding a project that can only fail. Because of the poor soils, there is no hope of success. Unlike the wealth we hope to create in the 80's based on an inclusive both/and approach to problems, where everyone gains from the solution, the Polonoroeste Project is an example of a lose/lose situation—the rainforests are cut down, presenting the threat of environmental disaster from which no one benefits as the soils are too weak to support a cropping system. Even if the real motives of the Brazilian government are not to help the poor peasant farmer, but to get them off the backs of the wealthy estate owners of the south, even these ignoble objectives will fail as tens of thousands of settlers, promised paradise by government television advertisements, find nothing but desolation.

The Polonoroeste Project shows all the signs of living in the past. The initiators of the project seem unaware that the pace of change in the world has made old ways of thinking and acting redundant, if not downright dangerous. They appear to be intimidated by change rather than its masters. How can we be sure of this?

The lose/lose situation they have boxed themselves into is the first sign of old, inappropriate behaviour. Taking the suggestions of Jonas Salk's analysis of changing values, projects helping to create a new stability have win/win outcomes. One project with such an outcome may be the work Lutzenberger reports being done at INPA, the Amazon Research Institute: '*Researchers there are showing that permaculture—trees such as breadfruit, jackfruit, and many other tropical fruit trees, coconut and numerous native palm trees—can produce up to ten times as much energy and protein per hectare (2½ acres) with less work, no new clearing, than the traditional crops can*'. In contrast then to the assured failure of the Polonoroeste Project, what are the benefits to this new win/win approach to the Amazon? To begin with, the rainforest would remain intact, Brazil increase its food output, ease the social unrest between peasant and estate owner in the south, and please Gaia at the same time. What's more, the cost would be nothing compared to the cost of the present destruction, and this would ease Brazil's crippling foreign debt.

Benefits like these will always elude the Polonoroeste Project which has not come to terms with the pace of change, or the new ways of thinking demanded by that change. The aims of the World Bank, major funders of the project, are '*to ensure growth of production in harmony with preoccupation for the preservation of ecosystems and natural resources*'. But because their view of development is not appropriate for the changing times, they are achieving the exact opposite of their intentions. The message for them is simple, either change, or fail.

How will Gaia respond to the crisis?

We don't know how Gaia will respond to this waste. Perhaps she can tolerate the destruction of her tropical forests as she has her temperate forests. But Lovelock warns us against complacency. Gaia, he suggests, will do the best for Gaia, and this may not always be what is best for man. If man is behaving like a cancer on her body, she may use her strength to cure this illness. The chilling television drama, *Edge of Darkness*, ends with the Earth covering her surface with tiny black flowers, absorbing heat from the sun and making life intolerable for man.

This may be science fiction, but all homeostatic systems have limits to their control, beyond which they breakdown. Lovelock suggests the regulation of the Earth's climate is not far from one of these limits.

He points out that the carbon dioxide levels cannot be reduced much below the levels around at the last period of glaciation without seriously limiting the growth of a vast number of plants. If the rainforests we're cutting down have a crucial role to play in global carbon dioxide feedback processes, we could be in trouble. The one thing that is clear is that we can't leave the solution to this dilemma to a handful of bank officials and government ministers. It is our survival that is at stake in the Amazon basin as much as anyone else's, but what can we do?

In search of survival

Political action through environmental pressure groups like Earthlife, Friends of the Earth, and Greenpeace are powerful ways of making ourselves heard at global dangerpoints throughout the world. And, as we have seen with the Polonoroeste Project, with its implicit aim of removing Brazil's poor away from the wealthy estate owners of the south, a new understanding of the relationship between the destruction of the environment and social injustice has made aid organizations like Oxfam strong forces for positive change. We in developed countries often underrate the influence we can have through organizations like these, but if you are ever in doubt just remember that the work of one man, Bob Geldof, raised £50 million ($71 million) in one night through Live Aid, the effects of which are still helping to restore the ecology of many famine stricken countries. You can find the addresses of many of these organizations at the back of this book.

But hand in hand with exercising our power for change through political action, the *Quantum Carrot* approach suggests another way we can start to work with Gaia and avert ecological disaster. This rests on a new 'systems' theory of health proposed by leading scientists and doctors. Work into cancer and heart disease is changing our whole concept of health, and how that health can break down to create illness. Previously many people have seen the destruction of the rainforests as possibly irreversibly damaging the biosphere's health. What is now becoming clear when we apply the new systems approach to health to the Earth as the largest living organism we know, is that deforestation *is a symptom of Gaia's ecological illness, rather than its cause*. The suggestion is that the destruction of the rainforest could be a sign of the Earth's feedback mechanisms beginning to breakdown *after already being weakened by other factors*.

Give Gaia a carrot

Lovelock suggests the destruction of the rainforests is all the more critical because Gaia's life support systems are already stretched to breaking point. Countless factors have operated to contribute to her illness, and weaken her defences. The rainforest destruction is only the straw that may break the camel's back. *'When such a system is stressed,'* says Lovelock, *'to near the limits of regulation even small disturbance may cause it to jump to a new stable state or even fail entirely'*.

With its desire to turn problems like these into opportunities, the Quantum Carrot approach gets to work increasing Gaia's vitality right across the globe, in any patch of garden, anywhere in fact that it can get its hands on, because the suggestion is that any improvement in Gaia's health at the local level will also increase the health of the whole system, bringing it back from the brink of breakdown. We may not have direct links with the World Bank, or live near enough to the Amazon to go and protect our wealth with our arms around the trees, but we have the power to increase the health of global life support systems wherever we are through small space organic gardening. This is some of the power that is available to us through *Quantum Carrot*.

We are not just talking about getting the soil right so our tiny friends can get down to their organic work. We are building health and vitality in the most highly developed systems life has yet evolved—ourselves. Our actions and our thoughts are the most powerful forces yet seen on Gaia. Filling these systems with life's vitality from the soil through small space gardening puts us right at the centrepoint of change. The pursuit of the new health-based wealth of the 80's puts us right where we can be most effective. The health we create here is also health to Gaia. And despite the controversy that surrounds the issue, freshly harvested organic vegetables can be one of the sources of that health, as they provide a source of nutrition that even the most advanced laboratory techniques available have yet to fully understand. Just how this happens is what we are going to look at next.

FIVE

Eat Organic!

```
┌─────────── TIPS FOR HIGH VITALITY ───────────┐
│                                               │
│   ★   eat organic!   ★   eat a 75% raw food   │
│  diet   ★   pick vegetables fresh as you need │
│  them   ★   create a rich variety of colour,  │
│  texture and flavour in your salads and       │
│  cooked dishes                                │
│                                               │
└───────────────────────────────────────────────┘
```

```
┌──── BENEFITS OF FRESH ORGANIC VEGETABLES ────┐
│                                               │
│  ★   pesticide free   ★   nitrate free   ★   │
│  full of nutrients in their right balance   ★ │
│  full of flavour   ★   good keeping quality   │
│  ★   high in 'structural information'         │
│                                               │
└───────────────────────────────────────────────┘
```

The vitality of organic plants is quite literally the pulse of life in its full splendour as it radiates from the sun, uncontaminated by poisons, or weakened through lack of soil nutrients. If you would like direct experience of this power try a glass of freshly made carrot and beetroot juice. I have found it to be one of life's most potent sources of energy, particularly if some wheat grass is also juiced at the same time. Details of how to grow all these plants are in the Gaiaculture section of this book. If you juice them yourself, you will soon see from their effect on your own vitality why organic juices like these are used all over the world by health clinics in the treatment of illness.

For us though, freedom from illness is no longer enough. In the *Quantum Carrot* adventure we are in search of a wealth based on high level health and well-being which will enable us to reach the peaks of our potential to live and enjoy life. The vitality of freshly harvested organic vegetables as part of the new 80's approach to life can help us reach those peaks. Sadly though, for the great majority of people in developed countries, such a life is little more than a dream. In fact, in the last years of the twentieth century, instead of a life of high health we seem to be cultivating degenerative disease—heart disease, hypertension, circulatory ailments, cancer, diabetes, arthritis, obesity, mental disorders. . . . Dr Robert Levy, director of America's National Heart, Lung and Blood Institute, reported that 35 million Americans suffer from high blood pressure, the primary cause of 1¼ million heart attacks and half a million strokes each year. At the same time, psychiatric authorities Bond and Menninger suggest that only 0.7% of Americans could pass as healthy in mind and spirit; the rest were struggling through life burdened unnecessarily with nervous obsessions and other prejudicial complexes. Instead of life on the peaks of well-being, many people are struggling just to survive. After 8,000 years of civilization this may seem absurd until we look at the reasons why.

Meso-health: just surviving

We've seen there are many factors that create disease—stress, psychological outlook, environmental factors and, perhaps most important of all, poor nutrition. Disease was previously thought of as the invasion of some harmful substance or microbe. But no such 'single cause' has been found for today's 'civilized diseases'. Bacteria, harmful to some people, do the rest of us no harm. Two people can be exposed to the same pesticide. A few years later one develops cancer, the other does not. What makes the difference? According to the new systems or environmental approach to health, a great deal depends on the overall health of our body system. Disease is the breakdown of the body's natural feedback mechanisms for sustaining health.

In the same way, a plant struggling for life in a lifeless, poisoned soil shows little resistance to the attacks of insects, fungi, or even changes in the weather like drought. It is struggling for survival, unable to grow to the fullness coded in its genes because it hasn't the resources to raise it to high-level health.

Like plants, people can survive at a low level of vitality if they are starved of proper nourishment. Even if they don't show clinical signs of illness, they are unable to function at their best, and are more vulnerable to harmful environmental influences. This is 'meso-health'—a state of half-hearted health induced by years of eating devitalised and processed foods.

In this 'twilight zone of ill health' as Swiss physician Max Bircher-Benner has called it, the body uses all its skill to adapt to working with the nutrition it has got, deprived of what it requires for fullness. Today this can continue for years, perhaps a lifetime, because we have become so accustomed to the tell-tale signs of meso-health that we accept them as part of the 'natural' ageing process. According to many doctors and researchers, many of us live in a state of meso-health most of the time. Take, for example, the three-year Health and Nutrition Examination Survey carried out in the United States between 1971 and 1974 on 28,000 people by congressional mandate. Even by highly conservative estimates it shows that half the women surveyed had calcium deficiencies; that iron deficiency was widespread among people of every race, income group and cultural background; and that more than 60% of those examined had at least one symptom of malnutrition. From this background of meso-health, what evidence is there that high level health is possible at all?

Tales from foreign lands

Like El Dorado, the fabled land of gold hidden away from the rest of the world, the first researchers looking at the link between health and nutrition found communities full of health that was undreamt of in our society.

Best known of these early pioneers was Sir Robert McCarrison who, while in the Indian Medical Service during the early part of this century, was deeply impressed by the health and vigour of certain of the races in the Northern Frontier region. In particular, the Sikhs and Hunzas suffered from none of the major diseases of Western nations such as cancer, peptic ulcer, appendicitis, and tooth decay. They were long lived, and their vibrant health was in marked contrast to the high morbidity of other races in the southern part of India.

Of major importance was McCarrison's discovery that the healthy northerners were expert farmers, maintaining the fertility of their soil organically. He also found that:

★ The bulk of their carbohydrates was in the form of wholegrain cereals; they ate no white flour and little or no sugar.

★ Much of their protein and fat came from an abundance of milk and milk products such as butter and cheese. Meat was only taken occasionally, about once a week.

★ This basic ration was supplemented by a wide variety of fruits and vegetables, often eaten raw.

★ Breast feeding was universal.

McCarrison later confirmed in a series of experiments as Director of Nutrition in India that for full health an organism needed food which was varied, fresh, unrefined, and free from artificial additives. Without such food, McCarrison repeatedly demonstrated that growth and stature were substandard, and resistance both to infection and degeneration lowered.

While McCarrison studied in India, the American dentist, Weston A. Price was travelling the world studying primitive societies—looking at the development of teeth and bones, the incidence of dental caries, and also the general physical and mental health of isolated cultures.

Where ever he went, Price found the same story. In his book *Nutrition and Physical Degeneration*, published in 1945, he carefully documented his findings, complete with photographs and statistics. His main conclusion was bleak; processed foods pose appalling dangers to human health. He argued that human health is related to the wholeness and freshness of the food we eat, and that a high level of health is almost impossible to achieve unless a diet is rich in uncooked foods. However, with the introduction of 'civilized food', the health of communities, like those studied by Price and McCarrison, rapidly deteriorates. In the 1956 Journal of the Women's Medical Association Dr Mary Jackson describes the rising incidence of dental decay, obesity, coronary disease, diabetes, and pregnancy toxaemia she observed among the Canadian Metis Indians after a new road to northern oil fields brought to these hunters and gatherers the processed foods of civilization. Findings such as these suggest that poor health, degenerative disease and premature ageing are the price we pay for civilization. But is there an alternative, even for those of us enmeshed in the stresses of post-industrial society?

Raw energy

A diet high in fresh, raw foods, free from poisons and containing the maximum vitality, is the menu for the highest level performance available. A full account of the amazing life-giving properties of raw foods is contained in Leslie and Susannah Kenton's book, *Raw*

Energy. I actually found myself transformed during its gestation from an invalid going through final exams and from a childhood of jelly and greasy sausages, to a much healthier person, able to run up the highest mountains in Britain. It showed me that a diet high in raw foods (their recommendation is about 75% of intake should be uncooked) was a way to a life of full health and a great deal of fun. The small space gardening techniques of Gaiaculture now make the amazing benefits of raw foods available to everyone. Indeed, *Quantum Carrot* complements the *Raw Energy* approach to health by providing the freshest and highest quality foods known to man, and reconnecting us to the source of that wealth, the Earth herself. What's more, garden fresh organic vegetables have special qualities of their own.

Quantum food doesn't kill you

Last year there were 14,000 cases of pesticide poisoning in the United States, and we have no idea of the burden these chemicals have put on our vitality and long-term health. Even the virility of the American male seems at stake due to environmental pollutants like DDT, reports Dr Ralph Dougherty at Florida State University, who has noticed a dramatic decline in sperm density of male semen. Last year a national survey of Australian farmers found at least one farmer in ten measurably poisoned by chemicals. With evidence like this, there can no longer be any doubt that pesticides pose a serious hazard to our health.

Organic foods are not one hundred percent free of pesticide residues, but they are a huge improvement on conventional produce, and certainly won't contain the outrageous pesticide levels, which in most countries exceed even official guidelines. For instance, in West Germany Professor W. Schuphan, founder of the former Federal Institute for Research on the Quality of Plant Produce, found pesticide residues in 37.7% of conventional vegetables analysed, but only in 3.2% of organic produce.

PESTICIDE RESIDUES IN CONVENTIONAL AND ORGANIC FRUIT AND VEGETABLES

Fruit & Vegetables	Conventional	Organic
Pesticide residue total (as % of total products)	37.7	3.2
Percentage over legal limit in West Germany	3.7	0

(Table from Schupbach in Vogtmann, 1981.)

Pesticide residues in organic vegetables are not there because organic growers are sneaking out and spraying their fields at night. Most of the residues are probably from spray drift from chemical neighbours. In the shelter of our homes and gardens, we should be harvesting vegetables of the highest possible purity. This same shelter can also help us avoid the now rapidly growing danger of nitrates from chemical fertilizers.

Goodbye nitrates

According to D. G. Steyn of the South African Department of Agricultural and Technical Services, of all the toxic residues in food, nitrates and their derivatives, nitrites, may constitute the greatest danger to health. Nitrate is converted to nitrite during the storage of vegetables, through our saliva when we eat, and when it comes in contact with the microbial action of our digestive system. Nitrites are the danger factor. In small children they can lead to 'blue-baby syndrome' (cyanosis) preventing oxygen uptake by the blood.

Today cyanosis is uncommon. More important is the dangerous property of nitrites when they combine with compounds called amines to form carcinogenic nitrosamines. All the ingredients nitrites need to form carcinogenic and even mutagenic compounds may be found in pesticides. Dithiocarbamate, a fungicide whose residues have increased in vegetables over the recent years, is one of the mixes for this sour cocktail.

Nitrates are often thought of as a problem in the water we drink, because of the vast amounts of soluble nitrogenous fertilizer from chemical agriculture that leaches through the soil to the water table each year. Certainly, the nitrate problem is directly linked to the excess of nitrogen fertilizers, but unbelievably, the average person in

54

Western Europe and North America obtains 70% of his daily nitrate intake from vegetables, and only 21% from water. In various areas there is a ban on drinking water for small children, but nitrate accumulation in vegetables, especially lettuce and spinach, is increasingly worrying.

In contrast to this nightmare Professor W. Schuphan has shown that organic foods on average contain sixteen times less nitrate-nitrogen than conventional crops, because they are not grown with large doses of soluble nitrogen fertilizer. The release of nitrogen by soil organisms is much more controlled, geared to the needs of the plant, avoiding the excesses of chemical application. However, the benefits of organic produce go far beyond just the mere absence of poisons.

Nutrient splendour

Sir Robert McCarrison followed up his observations of the Hunza and Sikh people with a series of experiments aimed at finding the secret of their high level of health. He discovered that rats fed on organic grain grew better and were more disease-resistant than those fed on grain produced with mineral fertilizers. The organic grain was also richer in vitamins. In other experiments, McCarrison found signs of higher vitality in organic crops resulting from a higher germation rate in organically grown seed than its chemical counterpart.

In 1938 the great European chemist Ehrenfried Pfeiffer described a number of experiments comparing bio-dynamic produce with mineral fertilized produce; in all cases bio-dynamic produce came out on top. The tests included egg production; egg hatchability and spoilage in chickens; germination of wheat after heating to 100°C (212°F); food preferences of mice when offered a choice of types of grain; and increased viability and disease resistance of turkey pullets. (Bio-dynamic agriculture is a form of organic growing based on the work of the educationist and mystic Rudolph Steiner.)

On a fresh weight basis, organic yields are often less than conventional crops. But don't be fooled. As one early potato grower once said to me 'we make a fortune selling water'. The dry matter content of organic foods is higher, concentrating nutrients. Schuphan has shown that although organic yields are 24% down on conventional crops, the dry-matter content averaged 23% more. But, impressive as they are, facts like these did not alone convince me of the nutrient splendour of organic foods.

It was the new sense of well-being I felt myself, combined with the results of many visits to organic farms. There I saw animals in full health, with clear eyes and shimmering coats. In particular the pedigree Welsh Black cattle of Plas Dwbl farm, Pembrokeshire, left me in no doubt of power of organic husbandry. Just the way they stood, with their eyes free from the anxiety now so common in most conventional herds, spoke of wealth and ease, their bodies unburdened by the stress of toxins or nutrient deficiency.

Conventional agriculture denies that well-being essential to farm animals and ourselves because soluble mineral fertilizers lock up valuable trace elements in the soil. It is now becoming clear that food is manufactured soil fertility. If the soil lacks essential elements, the quality of our food will be diminished. High levels of nitrogen fertilizer can make crops susceptible to infections like rust, powdery mildews and blasts. Van Nerum and Scheys reported at the Proceedings of the 12th Colloquium of The International Potassium Institute: *'We have been able to show that certain symptoms known to be due to microbial attack can also be caused by nutrient imbalance. Defective nutrition can render the plant more susceptible to microbial attack'*. How is a weak, sickly plant supposed to fill you with a vitality it hasn't got? Don't be fooled by outer appearances, the potatoes from your organic garden leave the competition standing, not only in terms of nutrients, but also in flavour.

Quality you can taste

Which one of us has not bought a beautiful rosy apple full of expectations of equally wonderful taste only to find ourselves chewing something similar to woodpulp? In contrast to quality based on visual appearance (the only standard for most conventional vegetables), organic gardeners use quality controls so high that very few storebought vegetables would pass—Nature's own signs of richness: aroma and flavour. A friend once gave me a few carrots from his chemical garden saying 'try these for quality and flavour'. I took them home and asked my family to compare them with carrots from my field. There was no comparison. To begin with you could hardly chew my friend's produce. In contrast the organic carrots were crunchy and sweet. Aaron, my little brother, even asked for more.

Other signs of organic excellence can only be seen under the microscope. At this level organically grown crops show very uniform cell structure, with strong cell walls in contrast to the weak, elongated shapes of cells force fed with artificial nitrogen. For us this cellular strength means our plants will withstand pests, disease, and the ravages of the weather much better than their chemical counterparts and will keep much better during the long winter months. Proof of better keeping quality has come from experiments by West German researchers E. Wistinghausen and B. D. Petterson. Their results show that even though conventional growers harvested a larger potato crop, after winter storage the organic crop had far fewer losses, and gave the higher yield, as well as higher starch content. And new research into the subtle qualities of living organisms is providing some unexpected ways in which we can understand the benefits of organic produce.

Brekhman's structural information

For instance, searching for a new way to measure the nutritional quality of foods, the Russian scientist I. I. Brekhman discovered that there was more to the nutritional quality of foods than the amount of calories they contained. In a series of experiments Brekhman noticed that rats fed on purified white sugar did less work than rats fed on raw molasses sugar—even though each sample of sugar had the same calorific value, the same amount of energy locked up in its structure. With further research Brekhman concluded that the enzymes and other substances not extracted from raw sugar contributed to the amount of energy available for the rats to use. The difference, he claimed, between refined and molasses sugar was that molasses contained more 'structural information', meaning that the molasses had a much greater variety and complexity of molecules than the very uniform makeup of refined sugar constructed from only a few molecules joined in the same pattern over and over again.

Living organisms, claims Brekhman, thrive on a rich abundance of the right kinds of structural information. In one sense, the greater the structural information, the greater life's force. For instance, an oil field has a high energy value when measured in calories, but even the simplest amoeba possesses greater structural information through the vast array of enzymes, nucleotides, and so on, which give it life. During the whole course of evolution organisms have evolved by becoming more and more complex, resulting in an ever increasing demand for more structural information. In relation to the food we eat, Brekhman claims that raw food is more life-giving than cooked or processed food because it contains much more usable structural information.

Experiments have not yet been carried out comparing the structural information of conventional and organic crops, but even a brief glance at their different growing environments suggests that one benefit of organic crops is that they are higher in such information. Why? Because from their germination organic plants grow in a living community of thriving complexity. The amount of structural information available for their growth far exceeds the inert wilderness that is home for their chemical cousins. We can profit from that increased structural information by ensuring we do not lack any of the 50,000 to 100,000 compounds that go into making and running our bodies.

But while research like Brekhman's is finding new ways to understand the subtle qualities of living organisms, there are simpler reasons to have your vegetables right at the kitchen door.

Fresh at the kitchen door

Lawrence D. Hills, organic gardener, author and head of the Henry Doubleday Research Association, points out that even if you buy only organic food supplied direct from an organic warehouse, it cannot be as fresh as produce that has only travelled the length of your garden path. All vegetables start losing vitamin C as soon as they are gathered, and the shorter the trip to the kitchen, the more vitamin C they retain. Other vital nutrients begin to decay soon after picking. I sometimes wonder what is left in an iceberg lettuce that has travelled half-way around the world to lie on my plate. Probably the pesticides. In the meantime, controversy still rages in the scientific community of the merits of conventional versus organic food.

Controversy, controversy

A Scientific Status Summary by the Institute of Food Technologies states, for example: *'Organically grown foods are identical in nutrition to those grown by conventional methods using inorganic chemicals. There is no scientific evidence that can demonstrate any difference'*. And researcher V. S. Packard writes in *Professional Nutritionist*: *'No nutrient differences exist in food crops grown under the two different methods—none. Those who suggest otherwise are clearly and grossly in error, whether purposely so or out of innocent ignorance.'*

A great deal of the argument comes from a lack of sound scientific evidence. There have been relatively few comparative studies, and many of the most recent have either been short-term, or without a clear understanding of what it is to grow organically. Organic growing is more than just the absence of chemicals, it is a forward-thinking technology designed to maximize the biological activity of the soil. This cannot be done overnight, or in the sterile isolation of a laboratory. Hopefully new long-term, farm-scale projects will provide a better scientific basis for understanding the differences between conventional and organic produce. But at its base, much of this controversy may be the result of two opposing worldviews—one based on a mechanical model of the universe that concentrates on units of production, and the other starting with an understanding of the Earth and her soils as one interpenetrating whole. And it may not be so much the results of research as a shift in worldview that will shed most light on the wealth organic produce can help us create.

SIX

The Quantum Link

In this crucial chapter, following the overview of the world we live in and preceding the practical small space gardening techniques of Gaiaculture, I would like to share a dream with you—a dream I believe we can make reality. That dream is a vision of a new wealth far beyond what we previously thought possible. The techniques of Gaiaculture are a way of reaping the high-life benefits of organic foods. But freedom from pesticides and nitrate contamination is not enough by itself to create the wealth we have been looking at. These threats which many of us have begun to battle against are only symptoms of the much greater issue—how we can escape the constraints of life-negating old habit patterns based on an obsolete world-view. It is this world-view which holds the greatest danger to our survival on this planet. It is also the limiting factor to creating the new wealth. Alter the world-view and we can quite literally transform our reality. But to make such a change we must rediscover within us the *power* to create a world we want to live in.

The old dualism

The Newtonian view of reality is based on classical dualism—the notion that mind and matter are separate. It owes much to Descartes' philosophy which divides reality into subject (I think) and object (I am). Such dualism made it possible for scientists to treat matter objectively, as something completely separate from themselves to be taken apart, analysed and catagorised. According to the mechanistic world-view based on the two-century-old physics of Newton, we have no power to transform our reality or to create the world we want to live in. We are only small cogs in the great universal machine. On the other hand, the world-view now developing from discoveries at the quantum physical levels of reality places human consciousness at the centre of the on-going process of creating the reality we live in. It tells us that the power for change rests quite literally within ourselves.

A Quantum Carrot approach to living suggests that the key needed to unlock this inner potential is the unlikely combination of the new quantum physical world-view with the down-to-earth practice of organic gardening. Why? Because without the shift in thinking proposed by the discoveries of quantum physics, the problems that face us appear to be without solution since we are not able to step beyond the no-win situations created by world-views now outdated by the pace of change. Yet just altering one's thinking is not enough. For the new quantum ways of thinking remain little more than a theory unless we translate them into our daily lives. Because of its close relationship with the Earth (the level at which change is now taking place), and its ability to produce high quality foods anywhere, the practical techniques of small space organic gardening are ideally suited as the first step towards putting this liberating world-view into practice. I have called this union between the insights of quantum physics and small space organic growing the Quantum Link. At its centre, like a bridge arched between the new ways of thinking and the new approach to gardening, we can now stand imbued with the power for positive change. The first step towards making this personal power a reality is to confront the choice we have between the two ways of living now presented to us by the exponential pace of change.

Across the threshold

The choice we are faced with is this: we can either continue to feel powerless and intimidated by the pace of change and remain trapped within old habit patterns whose only likely outcome is the failure of personal and environmental well-being, or we can step beyond these constraints and acknowledge the opportunities to create the life we choose through radical new ways of living. As never before we also stand at a threshold between two worlds, one leading us right to the edge of global failure, poor health, and despair, while the other promises new order at a higher level of stability, wealth and well-being than may never before have been possible.

How can we make this choice? Many people have already done so. For instance, a small but growing number of farmers and growers have discarded the outdated chemical approach to agriculture, and adopted new, liberating, organic practices based on a different world-view that they believe has the ability to solve the food crisis, and to create a lifestyle they find comfortable. A sign of the power unleashed by this new perspective is that organic farming is now the fastest

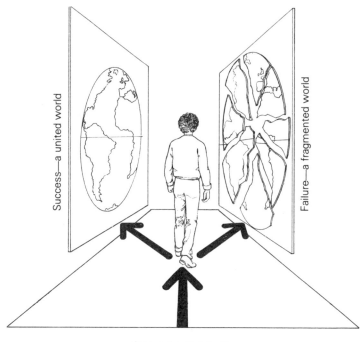

Across the threshold

growing sector of British agriculture. It now has the ability to lobby for agricultural reform far greater than its size would suggest. As fixed as our lives may at first sight appear, we each have the opportunity to step out of old habit patterns and unleash our own potential for positive change—an opportunity that comes from the growing awareness of the strength that a person's world-view has to condition the world in which they live.

The opening

In his book, *Towards a Science of Consciousness*, health researcher and author Kenneth R. Pelletier summarizes the growing scientific awareness of the power of a person's world-view to condition reality: *'In modern sciences ranging from the neurophysiology of consciousness to quantum physics, it is evident that the structure of an individual's personal belief system concerning the self and the universe governs that person's experience. . . . An immediate implication of this circumstance is that it is possible for an individual, by reformulating his belief system, to become aware of a vast realm of new possibilities.'* This ability is not just for the select few. We all have the power to open ourselves to freedom of new world-views. But perhaps even now, few of us realize to just what extent the problems that face us today are the result of the world-view of Newtonian physics.

Newton's universe

In its own time the Newtonian world-view has been indispensable for progress in scientific understanding, rapid industrialization and technological advance that has marked the last two centuries. It is not the Newtonian world-view itself that is dangerous; it has only become so because it is no longer appropriate to today's fast changing world. Indeed, taken as one option, rather than an exclusive way of looking at things, its analytical methods are still a very useful approach to problems in fields as diverse as understanding the functions of the brain, to the manufacture of components—or even just trying to fix the lawnmower.

But in its exclusive role as the *only* way of looking at things, the Newtonian world-view is not only leading us into possible global disaster, it is also the greatest single obstacle to the new health-based wealth we hope to create for ourselves. This is because the wealth we want to create can no longer be gained through exploitive or exclusive ways of thinking which are the outcome of the materialistic world picture painted by Newton. For instance, vegetables of the highest quality and free from toxic residues cannot be grown on land whose fertility has been exploited for the sake of individual profit alone. Only through a close relationship with the soil, where the gardener works to increase its biological activity, can there be any hope of the personal wealth we now seek. The exclusive approach of *either* soil fertility *or* profit just does not allow for the possibility suggested by new ways of thinking that we can have *both* soil fertility *and* still make a living, or even that this inclusive approach is in fact *essential* for vegetables of the quality we seek.

Of even greater importance, the frustration and feelings of powerlessness which many of us feel when faced with the problems of daily survival (which only lead to anger or depression and a sense of futility) are not true representations of our individual power and autonomy, but the result of our identifying with the Newtonian world-view which denies individual power through a sense of subject/ object isolation from the world, and belittles our freedom through ever-present laws of gravity and motion which leave no room for individual desire. If the world we live in were only the combinations of matter in motion suggested by Newton (a world which denies any power to our wishes) then these feelings of frustration and powerlessness would be fully justified. From such a point of view practically every threat to our well-being—from the destruction of rainforests to additives permitted in our foods—is beyond our effective control. It is only by stepping beyond this limiting picture onto a quantum level that we can awaken a power for change, a power being experienced today by a growing number of people. It is that step across the threshold of the old into the new that is the choice we face.

Turning on the power

This sense of the choice between two world-views presented itself to me while working on my land. Engrossed in the ebb and flow of life through the seasons it gradually dawned on me that, like Nature, our lives are often a process of giving up what we have got in order that we may have more. There is nothing mysterious in this, it is just how the biological process works. Nature could not burst forth in spring if she had not let go of the fruits of previous summers. In the same way, the power we seek to build a new wealth for ourselves can only come when we are able to let go of old habit patterns, misplaced conceptions of ourselves and the world we live in—in fact, letting go of all that is no longer useful so that we can embrace the new. Like a catapult drawn back ready to fire, the pace of change in our lives today has created a state of tension which can provide the impetus to release this power from within us if only we let go of old habits. If we cannot let go, then it is likely that these tensions will quite literally take us to the breaking point.

But what exactly is this power we seek? What force has strength to overcome the crisis that faces our Earth, let alone create a new order from the impending darkness? As I harvested my new potatoes and bunched summer carrots for market, the belief grew within me that that force must be life itself. For life has a strength even greater than the unleashed power of the atom bomb. For unlike the bomb, life's power can be used to create. The bomb can only destroy. Consider for a moment the potential of the power on whose threshold we stand. For example, where the most advanced laboratory analyses have failed to clarify the exact dangers from taking in the daily combination of toxic chemicals in our environment, organic soil life creates foods that help protect us from harm. And what force have we yet developed that can raise the ecology of the planet to a new level of stability? Certainly not our most sophisticated computers, which stand dwarfed next to the intricacy of Gaia's living feedback mechanisms. All of these things made me realize that if only we are able to connect to life's pulse, we could begin to experience and work with the greatest surge in power since we unlocked the secrets of the atom—and, according a growing number of scientists, far more beneficial.

Searching for a way to make this connection, we do not have to look far since life's force lies at the heart of our own being. We are one of the most sophisticated biological organisms on Earth—a highly evolved concentration of living energy. And to make the power work for us we have only to do two things: first we must acknowledge its presence, and then we must align ourselves with this living strength. Insights from quantum physics can help us experience that presence. Working with life's currents and harvesting its splendours through small space gardening is the easiest way of all to align ourselves with life-creating force. *Has there ever been a better time to look beyond the old into the world of the new?*

Changes in world-views

By contrast with the isolated and powerless individual of the Newtonian world-view, quantum physical research paints a picture of consciousness as the decisive factor in the unfolding of our everyday world. Its findings show that, at its most fundamental levels, reality is nowhere near as simple as Newton thought. Newton gave precise laws for the world we see, smell, taste, touch and hear. But according to quantum physical theory, the fragmented world of atoms and molecules is only a *secondary* reality—a reality which has been unfolded from the deeper realm of possibility which underlies all form. According to British physicist David Bohm, deepest reality lies *behind* the observable realm. It is a reality integrated as an indivisible whole beyond the boundaries of space and time—a wholeness to which we belong and from which our power for positive change springs. Bohm calls this deeper reality *the implicate order*—the realm of no divisions, no fragmentation, only the undivided wholeness from

TWO WORLD-VIEWS COMPARED

Old ways of thinking	*New ways of thinking*
NEWTONIAN PHYSICS	QUANTUM PHYSICS

Approach to the world:

explicit fragmentation	implicit unity
atomistic	holographic
fixed laws of motion	fields of possibility

Approach to the individual:

machine	organism
mind/body split	mind/body unity
matter	consciousness

Approach to problem solving:

exclusive	inclusive
either/or	both/and

Source of power:

energy	synergy
limited potential	the power of limits
entropy	creative power

Source of wealth:

material attachment	personal bonding

Nature of change:

continuous	discontinuous
uniform	quantum leaps

which our everyday world, or *explicate order*, unfolds. '*Wholeness is what is real*', says Bohm, opening up a realm of personal initiative that would have been difficult to imagine before.

Why? Because despite the fragmentation of the manifest world all around us, where I am just one individual among many billions, and nations divide the Earth, it is not this fragmentation which is real. At a fundamental level of my being I am intimately connected to all other aspects of my world. Instead of interacting with just my immediate surroundings as suggested by the atomistic world-view of Newton, at the implicate level I participate with the Earth as a whole. It is this bonding with our world that gives us the power to transform—in the same way a potter would mould his clay, we have direct access to the world we want to change.

Previously, according to the Newtonian world-view, all our actions appeared to make very little difference to the world at large as they were bound by the fixed laws of gravity and motion. These laws give strict limits to our power to influence. Now, instead of a fixed universe, we find ourselves working with fields of possibility that unfold according to our own thoughts and desires. Because, just as the potential of the implicate order needs the constraints of the Newtonian universe in order to manifest as positive change, the changes in our world-view brought by the insights of quantum physics are only useful if we translate their potential into the practical task of creating a new wealth for ourselves through day to day techniques like small space organic gardening. It is this connection between the possibilities opened to us through the insights of quantum physics, and practical improvements to our health, vitality and lifestyle through techniques like small space organic gardening that are the Quantum Link.

Living genius

As the focal point of the Quantum Link we are at the centre of the power this fusion can create—a power which is quite literally life itself. Free from outdated conceptions of ourselves as complex machines built out of the components of a liver, heart, brain and so on, such new ways of thinking have brought a conception of ourselves as living systems which differ in exciting ways to that of a machine. One is the ability of living systems to create order out of chaos. In total contradiction to the Newtonian world of inanimate matter slowly grinding down towards a state of uniform energy called entropy, living systems use order to build highly sophisticated concentrations of complexity and energy—like our own bodies. We all know how our new car soon begins to show signs of entropic decay as the bodywork begins to rust and the valves wear out, while we as living systems replace most cells in our bodies every few months. People who continue to associate themselves with the outdated image of themselves as a machine find that their power is limited by that image because their world-view does not allow for the remarkable talents of living systems to create greater

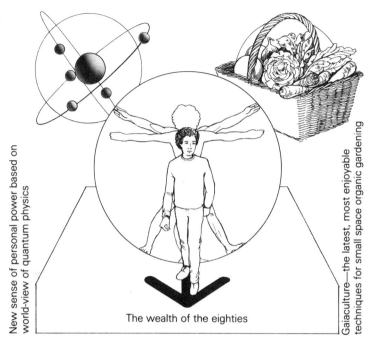

New sense of personal power based on world-view of quantum physics

Gaiaculture—the latest, most enjoyable techniques for small space organic gardening

The wealth of the eighties

The quantum link

order out of chaos. Organic gardening is the way *Quantum Carrot* suggests we use the power that only living systems have to concentrate order and energy so that we may raise our own vitality *and* that of the Earth. And once real transformation has begun, against all the logic of linear progression, the changes living systems make do not just plod along, they take place in quantum leaps and bounds.

Quantum leaps

Imagine for a moment the splendour that could come if Gaia made a discontinuous leap on a global scale. And imagine how great you would feel if you made that same leap to a higher level of health and well-being. Small scale gardening is one of the most important and easily accessible ways we can work with Gaia so together we can make the discontinuous leap for wholeness, health and creativity—a leap that only living systems can make.

This tantalizing possibility comes from the 'rooth monkey' story, based on the research observations of a group of scientists studying the behaviour of a group of monkeys on a remote Japanese island. As part of the study, the scientists left potatoes as food for the monkeys, which were readily eaten even though they were often covered with soil. One day, the scientists noticed one young monkey take its potato down to the nearby stream and wash away the soil before eating it. This continued for a number of days, after which the young monkey taught its parents and other close relatives the same technique. In the following days this slowly spread throughout the group as one monkey taught another. Up to that point the spread of learning had been continuous, uniform and based on individual example. But the next day the scientists returned and found the entire monkey population of the island washing their potatoes before eating them. Not only that, but at the same instant, monkey colonies on other distant islands had adopted the same behaviour, even though it had never been observed in those colonies before. Baffled, scientists had to look towards the new concepts of quantum physics for an answer.

In an attempt to understand what had happened they suggested that at a certain critical 'threshold', (after a certain number of monkeys had learnt the technique), the process of transmission shifted in a single leap from localized behaviour, to take on a non-local, universal power. Not all monkeys had to learn by example—as long as the critical threshold was reached, there was a discontinuous leap in the power of the group to alter their behaviour.

Quantum leap

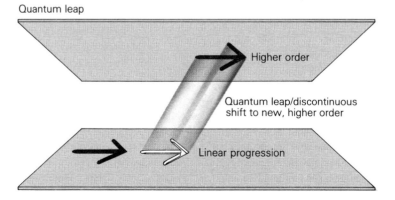

It seems probable that other living systems, including ourselves, have the same ability to participate in discontinuous shifts in evolution, which could have important consequences for us. If techniques like those described in this book become available to enough of us, this may help precipitate a quantum shift in Gaia's health onto a new level of vitality. And for ourselves, the organic vegetables we harvest can help us make our own discontinuous leap to a new level of health where we can start enjoying a richer, fuller life.

This has certainly happened to me. After a few months on a diet high in raw food and plenty of organic vegetables, I still suffered terrible aches and pains in my back and shoulders when I ran. But then, almost overnight, they disappeared. And once they had gone, I found that even after days without high quality foods my running still went well—I had made a discontinuous leap in well-being and stabilized at a new level of health. Of course, I am sure it was not just organic foods that made this shift possible, but combined with other improvements in my lifestyle and psychological outlook. Yet for me, organic foods were the trigger that enabled me to reach the critical threshold needed to make that leap. It is a higher level of being which is the basis of the new concept of wealth we have talked so much about—wealth based on health, personal power, and autonomy for ourselves and the Earth. Indeed, by starting to create this new wealth, we are already beginning to use our potential as living systems to the full. The insights of quantum physics have suggested a new way of looking at things that makes this fullness possible, and hints at the power we have to initiate positive change in our own lives. Armed with the *Quantum Carrot*, let us now look at the practical ways to bring that fullness into our homes and vegetable patch with the latest techniques of small space organic gardening.

PART TWO - GAIACULTURE

Right, let's start growing. Gaiaculture is your practical, user-friendly guide to organic growing in the simplest ways possible. We are going to start right from scratch, like absolute beginners. But if you already know what you want, skip to the other chapters and get stuck in.

As far as possible Gaiaculture is based on my own practical experience, and the experience of my organic gardening friends. You will quickly find there are as many ways to garden as there are gardeners. Growing is practical, it can not be tied down by rules and regulations. Each one of us will bring something special and unique to cultivating the Earth. For instance, weeds are usually bad news—'one year's seeding is seven years' weeding'—but last winter one grower found weeds protected his carrots against vicious frosts while everyone else lost their crops. Again, crop rotation is an essential way of maintaining soil health and pest control, but Mal, who gardens organically in Pembrokeshire, has grown onions on the same plot of land year after year and still gets excellent results.

Part of the excitement of growing is finding that uniqueness for yourself. Gaiaculture is your sourcebook for those general guidelines which have been found to work in the past, and your troubleshooter if blackfly are ravaging your broad beans, or wireworm sculpting your new potatoes. But your soil type, where you live, your climate, shelter from the wind, sunlight . . . indeed a whole host of factors are going to determine your own unique approach to organic gardening. And the most important factor is YOU. You are the star of the show, the essential ingredient for success, so let us start there.

SEVEN

Guidelines for Success

In keeping with the win/win approach to problems we have looked at in Earthcrisis, over the past few years of organic growing I have come to realize that we produce the best crops when we garden in a way that does the best for us. Here are some suggestions I have found useful to keep me on the path to organic success.

GAIACULTURE'S GUIDELINES FOR SUCCESS

★ the most important factor is YOU ★ grow together ★ take it easy ★ keep it simple ★ grow only vegetables you like

---

Grow together

After years of heroic single-handed efforts to weed never-ending rows of carrots, and ending with nothing but frustration, desperation and failure, I decided to change my ways. Why, I thought, am I growing on my own when it might be more rewarding to share the work with others? Sure enough it was. I have never laughed so much as when weeding the same carrots with Susannah my sister, and with other friends. Planting 5,000 cabbages one hot, dusty afternoon turned into one of the best parties I have ever been to. And one summer I had half the village children helping me harvest, weed, and plant. Occasionally the job was not the most professional I have ever seen, but it was far more fun working with other people. My old way of doing things was to walk out in the morning and see how much work I could manage before I died of either boredom or exhaustion. It was not a very pleasant way of working, and I never accomplished half of what I set out to do.

In contrast, people make anything possible, and they make it fun.

Yes, there are times when I like being on my own, washing out my sprouts, or harvesting the first new potatoes. Sometimes gardening becomes a form of meditation, my communion with the Earth. If you have been surrounded by people all day, maybe all you will want is to be out amongst your carrots on your own. It will ground you again, centre your energies so that you feel restored. That is part of what Gaia can do for you. The size of the plot is irrelevant. My indoor tomato and lettuce plants are sometimes the only companions I need. The American Indians call trees 'the standing people', and I have found plants can take on those same qualities.

But there is another reason to involve others in Gaiaculture—I have picked up my best gardening tips not just from reading books, but by 'talking shop' with farmers in their fields, doctors in their surgeries, strangers in their allotments, and high flying executives at plush dinner parties. Gaiaculture is full of their wisdom. You can gather your own gems practically wherever you are, whoever you are with—it is a way of sharing the great organic conspiracy of creating a new wealth and having fun.

Take it easy

At first my initial enthusiasm for organic growing threw me into projects larger than I could handle. I also thought it was only worthwhile growing if I could do it on a large enough scale. After many failures I now know that size has nothing to do with the success we are talking about in *Quantum Carrot*. In fact, any time when organic gardening stops being a pleasure and becomes a labour, stop. *You are the most important ingredient for success. If you don't feel good, Gaiaculture is not doing you good.* Sweating blood and tears is a sign we are back in those old habit patterns that say work is a toil, and if we are not suffering we are not getting anywhere. From the perspective of the new approaches to problem solving discussed in Earthcrisis this is ridiculous. Success will now come to the extent we let it. Gaiaculture cannot help us create a sense of well-being if we are feeling irritable and grumpy because we have 'had to weed the onions and plant out the cabbages'. Nature takes pleasure in the abundance she produces. It is no hardship for earthworms to enrich your soil, or for mycorrhizal fungi to interweave with the roots of your plants. Her pace is measured for success. She never asks more of her creation than they will gladly give.

Keep it simple

Some gardening books are full of descriptions of the most convoluted methods of growing. They are impossible to understand, let alone perform. Others produce complex cropping guides giving the best combination of vegetables to maximize crop output fanatically per square inch of ground. In contrast Gaiaculture keeps things as simple as possible, because it believes this is the best and most exciting way to get results. The complexity of *Quantum Carrot* is an intricacy no gardening book could hope to describe—the life of the soil and the power of Gaia.

Doctors Barbara and Gordon Latto have one of the most beautiful gardens I have ever seen which provides most of the food for themselves and the hundreds of guests that drop by each year. Their methods of growing are very simple, based around the compost heap and a simple rotation, which has been creating wealth for years. Both lead very busy lives and don't have the time to get involved in horticultural acrobatics. They do what works, and what splendour comes from it!

Grow what you like

Just because most rotations include brassicas (the cabbage family), this does not mean you have to grow cabbage. I personally hate the stuff and would not waste my space growing something neither my family or I would eat,. That is my own individual preference. What do you absolutely adore? What makes your mouth water just at the thought? Whatever it is, why not grow it?

A few years ago many people sat down to a Sunday dinner of 'meat and two veg'. Today our eating habits have changed enormously. Shops are stocking exotic fruits and vegetables unheard of before. In the same way we can experiment with what we grow. We are not limited to lettuce, potatoes, swede (rutabaga) and cabbage. Most seed companies stock new vegetables—cherry tomatoes, sugarloaf chicory, red lettuces. New vegetable seeds arrive from other countries each year—Italian chicories, fennels, and many cut-and-come-again lettuce varieties, to name only a few. All this adds up to a totally new freedom of choice of what to grow. Experiment and make the most of Nature's diversity.

On the other hand, I've just discovered how delicious grated swede (rutabaga) is in a winter salad—traditional vegetables lose none of their flavour just because they have been around for years. And they have the added benefit that you know they are suited to your climate.

With all this choice, you and your family are the crucial factor in the equation. What do *you* want to grow? What do *you* want to eat? Crops you like will flourish in your garden because of the extra care you give them. And that is just as appropriate to the organic splendour we can create inside our own homes, the subject we now turn to.

I   THE INDOOR GARDEN

How to grow where no one has grown before

EIGHT

Absolute Beginners

All the benefits of organically grown fresh food are now available to you for less than two minutes a day through sprouted seeds and grains—young plants in their first stages of growth. Their exotic shapes, sizes, flavours, colours and textures offer far more than tasteless store-bought mung bean shoots, and can be grown for only a fraction of the cost. These are probably one of the richest foods known to man. Some of the easiest sprouts are: mung beans, lentils, fenugreek, chick peas, marrowfat peas, mustard, radish, cress and wheat. Start with a few of these, and graduate to: alfalfa seeds, aduki beans, sunflower seeds, pumpkin seeds, sesame seeds, buckwheat, most beans and peas, almonds, rye, oats, tricitale, millet and rice. (Remember kidney beans are poisonous if eaten raw.) Buy your seeds from a store with a fast turnover.

A guide to sprouting

One handful of seeds will make about four handfuls of sprouts, so use a jar that can cope with the increase.

Rinse the seeds and pick out any small stones. Soak overnight, and in the morning rinse again, leaving the seeds moist, but not lying in water. Rinse them twice a day in a sieve and then return them to their jars. Cover the top of the jars with mesh, held in place with an elastic band. (I use the plastic mesh used to reduce sunlight in greenhouses, but any gauze will do.) Twice a day fill the jars with water, shake, pour out, and leave slanted on the draining board to drain.

Sprouts grow faster in the dark, but anywhere with moderate warmth and out of direct sunlight will do. Harvest according to the sprouting chart (reproduced from Leslie and Susannah Kenton's *Raw Energy*). Sprouts will keep for up to a week in the fridge, rinsed and sealed in a plastic bag.

SPROUTING CHART

Small seeds (soak 6–8 hrs)   T = tablespoon   c = cupful

	Dry amount to yield 1 litre/1¾ pints	Ready to eat in	Length of shoot (approx.)	Growing tips	Notes
Alfalfa	3–4T	5–6 days	3.5cm (1½in)	Taste particularly good after a day in sun-light.	Rich in organic vitamins and minerals.
Fenugreek	½C	3–4 days	1cm (½in)	Have quite a strong 'curry' taste.	Good for ridding the body of toxins.
Mustard no soaking needed	¼C	4–5 days	2.5cm (1in)	Can be grown on damp paper towels for at least a week; the green tops are cut off and used in salads.	Mustard is known as a counter-irritant and health tonic.
Radish no soaking needed	¼C	4–5 days	2.5cm (1in)	Taste just like radishes! The red hot flavour is great for dressings, or mixed with other sprouts in salads.	Radish is particularly good for clearing mucus and healing mucous membranes.
Sesame	½C	1–2 days	Same length as seed	If grown for longer than about 48 hours sesame sprouts become very bitter.	Sprouting makes sesame more digestible and its nutrients (lots of calcium and vitamin E) more readily available.

Larger seeds (soak 10–15 hrs) T = tablespoon c = cupful

	Dry amount to yield 2 litres/3½ pints	Ready to eat in	Length of shoot	Growing tips	Notes
Aduki beans	1½C	3–5 days	2.5–3.5cm (1–1½in)	Have a nutty 'legume' flavour.	Especially good for the kidneys.
Chick peas	2C	3–4 days	2.5cm (1in)	May need to soak for about 18 hours to swell to their full size. Renew water twice during this time.	Chick peas are a good source of protein and therefore helpful in body building for people who are underweight.
Lentils	1C	3–5 days	½–2.5cm (¼–1in)	Try different kinds. They are good eaten young or up to about 6 days old. 'Split' lentils will not sprout.	A staple food throughout the world—form a complete protein with rice and other grains.
Mung beans	1C	3–5 days	1–5cm (½–2½in)	Soak at least 15 hours. Keep in the dark for a sweet sprout. Put a weight (plastic bag filled with water and tied) on the beans to get long straight sprouts.	One of the most popular sprouts and one of the easiest to grow.
Sunflower	4C	1 day	Same length as seed	Can be grown for their greens. Bruise easily, so handle with care. Bitter if sprouted for more than 24 hours.	An excellent food—supplies the entire body with valuable nutrients.

Grains (soak 12–15 hrs)   T = tablespoon   C = cupful

	Dry amount to yield 1 litre/1¾ pints	Ready to eat in	Length of shoot	Growing tips	Notes
Wheat	2C	2–3 days	Same length as grain	A delicious sweet sprout with many uses including wheat grass and rejuvelac (the soak water). Large quantities are needed for breads.	An excellent source of the B vitamins. The soak water can be drunk straight, added to soups and vegetable juices, or fermented.
Rye	2C	2–3 days	ditto	Has a delicious distinctive flavour.	Good for the glandular system.
Barley	2C	2–3 days	ditto	As with most sprouts, barley becomes quite sweet when germinated.	Particularly good for people who are weak or underweight.
Oats soak 5–8 hrs only	2C	3–4 days	ditto	You need whole oats or 'oat groats'.	Like other grains, lose much of their mucus-forming activity when sprouted.
Millet soak 5–8 hrs only	2C	3–4 days	ditto	Must be unhulled millet, not couscous.	The only grain that is a complete protein and alkaline.

NINE

New Beginnings

The indoor garden brings quality into your home. For me that quality starts with the beauty of plants, whether that is the translucent quality of a lettuce leaf, or the red richness of ripe tomatoes spilling over the brim of a hanging basket. Like houseplants, but faster growing, indoor gardening transforms the atmosphere of a room or flat. This happens quite literally as the plants breathe, taking in carbon dioxide, and giving out moisture and oxygen. Remember what it feels like to walk into a wood on a hot summer's day and feel the cool, rich, almost scented atmosphere of the trees? Farmers know how a wood can change local weather conditions, keeping the air moist and cool. Indoor gardening starts to create that same luxury in your own home—you are creating your own living world. And, like sprouts, the indoor garden can bring you fresh vegetables at times of high prices in the stores. The first step towards this indoor wealth is getting your young plants started.

Should I buy my plants?

Most gardening books are against buying in plants because of the risk of bought in disease like clubroot in cabbages. But I have had few problems, and, faced with the realities of one's lifestyle, young lettuce or tomato plants from the local garden centre may be the best way to get started. Admittedly, they probably have not been started organically, but perhaps at this stage it is more important to get your garden flourishing than to be too dogmatic. After all, they will still spend most of their lives under organic conditions.

If you are buying plants, do not accept rubbish. Long, drawn out lettuce seedlings will never recover. Usually the smaller the plants, the better. Go to a reputable dealer, and make sure all plants look strong and healthy with no mildew, or strange creatures crawling all over them. Only tomato plants should look slightly anaemic and drawn— with a little stress they produce more tomatoes and less growth. But if you have time to germinate your own seeds (which can be one of the most exciting parts of gardening, watching life unfold from apparently lifeless seeds), three different methods are available according to the vegetable variety, and your own individual needs. Details of potting composts are in the Fertilizer chapter.

Three ways to sow

The way you sow depends on what you are growing:

Broadcasting For tiny plants tightly packed together like mustard, or some lettuce varieties, simply sprinkle the seeds thinly in a compost filled saucer, pot or tray where they are going to grow.

Station planting Large seeds like marrows, courgettes (zucchini), beans and peas can all be sown by putting single seeds exactly where we want them. That may be one courgette seed in each 7.5cm (3in) pot to get them started before potting them on to a larger container or hanging basket, or a dozen runner beans in a 45.5cm (18in) diameter pot to trail over a balcony. Smaller seeds can also be sown this way. For instance, you may want to sow just three lettuce a week to keep your flat supplied all summer. Just put two seeds direct into three 10cm (4in) pots. When the seeds germinate, prick out the weaklings, leaving the strongest to grow on.

Seed tray germination and pricking out is for large numbers of plants, especially if the seeds are small. These are sown into a seed tray and pricked out into containers when the plants are large enough to handle. This is the way nurserymen start summer bedding plants we buy for our garden borders. The process is a little more complicated than either broadcasting or station planting, and cannot be used with some vegetables. For instance, most root crops (including carrots, beetroot and parsnips) will not stand transplanting. It will fork their roots, or make them bolt. Swiss chard, spinach, swede (rutabaga), radish and turnip are the same. Indoors it is best to sow these seeds by station planting. So reserve seedtray germination for stubborn seeds and large numbers of plants.

All these germination methods use the following guidelines:

1 Choose the right size container for the job and fill with potting compost. If using a seedtray, fill with 2.5–4cm (1–1½in) of compost.
2 Gently level the surface with your hand, making sure all the corners are filled. Firm down.

3 Sprinkle the seeds very thinly over the surface of the compost, or press the seeds in at the desired spacing if you are station planting.

4 Cover with a thin layer of compost, between 0.25–0.5cm (⅛–¼in) depending on the size of the seed and gently firm down with your hand.

5 Water, either with a fine spray watering can so as not to disturb the compost, or by soaking the pot or seedtray in a saucer for a few minutes to let the compost absorb water through capillary action. You should not have to water again until the seeds have germinated.

6 Place in a propagator with the ventilation holes closed to stop the soil from drying out, or just as effective, cover with a plastic bag or sheet of glass. Black plastic will help retain moisture, absorb heat and keep light out which will encourage germination.

7 Keep warm, between 13°–16°C (55°–65°F) for most plants. If you do not have a plant propagator, airing cupboards, gas ovens with pilot lights, or next to a radiator are other good locations.

8 Then check each day for signs of life and to make sure the compost has not dried out. Most seeds will germinate in 3–14 days.

9 As soon as they are up, seedlings need a new environment for healthy growth. First they need light and secondly air. Remove the black plastic and any other coverings so that the seedlings can breathe. Open ventilation holes on propagators. Young seedlings will not stand direct sunlight, but they need plenty of light if they are not to become straggly and drawn.

10 Water like a miser. One of the biggest problems with young seedlings is a fungal disease called Botrytis, or 'damping off', especially in cool, damp spring and autumn sowings. It attacks young plants, leaving patches of dead plants in your seedtray. The only remedy is prevention by keeping the soil on the verge of drying out, good sunlight and constant airflow over the plants. Damping off will not affect larger seeds.

Pricking out

If you have used the seedtray method of germination and need to transplant your seedlings into a larger container, prick them out as soon as they are large enough to handle. The earlier the better, before their roots become intertwined into a thick mat at the bottom of the seedtray. The growth of seedlings will not be checked if they are pricked out young.

Do this by taking some of the young plants and lay them on the counter. Hold a seedling by its leaves (not the stem as this could injure it), and gently tease out its roots from the compost with a sharp pencil. Dibble a hole into new pot and lower the roots in. Gently firm down so the seedling stands upright.

Pricking out seedlings

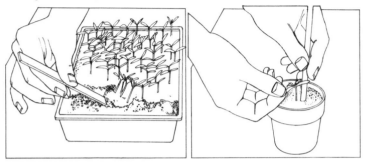

Gently lift seedling from tray

Place in dibbled hole and gently firm down

Potting on

Plants destined for large pots, tubs, growbags or hanging baskets, like tomatoes and courgettes (zucchini), prefer a smaller, 7.5cm (3in) pot as an intermediate stage. When they are 10–12.5cm (4–5in) high, transfer them again to their final growing positions. For this last move half fill the larger pot with compost. Turn the plant upside down and tap the bottom of the pot, and it should come free in your hand. Place the plant in its new home and pack it in with more potting compost. Water well.

Hardening off

If plants are going outside on a balcony, or a window box, they need to become acclimatized to the different environment. As soon as the plants are large enough to be planted in their final growing positions, put them outside during the day and bring them in at night to harden them off. After a week the plants should be used to their new environment and can be left outside.

Frost sensitive plants like courgettes (zucchini), tomatoes and runner beans can only be hardened off in late spring when the last risk of frost has hopefully gone.

If possible, all your indoor garden plants appreciate days outside in good weather when they are young. It thickens their cell walls and makes them more resistant to disease. Even later on, they would delight in a day outside and a good wash by summer showers. Failing that, they will settle for a good spring clean with all the windows open on warmer days.

Successful tips for the indoor garden

Here are a few things I have found useful in dealing with the special needs of indoor plants.

Grow together   Like people, plants seem to do best grown together. Two lettuce side by side grow better than one on its own. Like the way trees create their own local environment in a forest, plants seem to do the same.

Give them light   Plants need good strong light. Without it they will become weak and drawn, unable to bear the fruits we want. We ask a lot more of indoor vegetables than ordinary houseplants. We expect them to grow faster, and adorn our table with rich crops. They are happy to oblige, but most need a good 6–10 hours a day of direct sunlight.

Air   Plants do not like stagnant air. It is like being stuck in the office too long. They appreciate good ventilation, at least once in a while, to renew their vigour.

Water in moderation   Waterlogging will cause damping off in young plants, and sour soil in large pots. Buy a moisture gauge, or feel the soil with your finger. If it is damp, no water is needed. All plants also like their leaves watered with a hand spray which seems to freshen them up. Do not spray delicate leaves in direct sunlight as this could scorch them.

Air conditioning will do nothing for plants except chill them. If you are lucky enough to live in a climate that needs air conditioning, grow all your crops outside in tubs, window boxes and hanging baskets.

Drainage keeps the soil life happy. Without drainage holes you have to be adept at getting the water right. Put broken crockery or pebbles in the bottom of all pots over 15cm (6in) in diameter to help drainage before filling with compost. This is essential in large tubs.

Feeding   A good potting compost in a pot large enough to allow strong roots will meet all the needs for most crops. However, liquid feeds sprayed on the leaves boosts production of all plants. Liquid seaweed is full of trace elements, hormones and vitamins from one or more species of seaweed. Add a small amount to your hand sprayer and let the leaves soak up the goodness.

Cats can decide pots and tubs make convenient toilets. If they become a problem, cover the soil with large pebbles or plastic netting so they cannot dig into the soil.

Going away   Large pebbles also help to conserve moisture that can stop a plant drying out if you are away for a few days. Moss is another attractive soil cover that prevents water loss.

Pests should, hopefully, be few and far between. Red spider mite, and aphids are probably the most common. We will deal with pests under each vegetable heading below, and in the chapter on Banishing Pests.

Weeds   Soil-less composts, or those with sterilized soil should contain no weed seeds at all. Pick out any weeds that do find their way in as soon as they germinate.

Troubleshooting   If you come across unexpected problems with your indoor garden, see what we would do with the same vegetable outside. That may give you more insight into the nature of the problem and how it can be solved.

What containers can we grow in?

I have grown indoors using five different kinds of containers but I am sure you can think of others that will make most use of your different home climates.

Pots are by far the largest category as they come in all shapes, sizes, colours and materials. Simple pots can be made cheaply out of old washing up liquid bottles or newspaper. Yoghurt pots 10cm (4in) in diameter are very good for baby greens. If you are broadcasting, you will need a shallow, large diameter pot, 30cm (12in) saucers (usually used as trays for large pots), 4cm (1½in) in depth are ideal. If you are station planting large plants like courgettes (zucchini), or pricking large plants out of seedtrays, put them into small 7.5cm (3in) pots first, and then pot them on to 20cm (8in), 30cm (12in) and larger pots later. These large plants will need a depth of at least 20cm (8in) to produce the extensive root system essential for organic growing. Most pots will need adequate drainage unless you are very careful about watering.

Tubs are ideal for patios or balconies. You can start your own designer gardens through the creative combination of different plants all growing together. How about a central crop of carrots surrounding tall sweetcorn, with an outer circle of bush tomatoes hanging over the side, interspaced with parsley, or marigolds to improve their flavour, add colour, and keep pests away? Treat wooden tubs with old engine oil instead of wood preservative which may poison your plants. Kitchen herb gardens thrive in tubs, but spreading plants like mint should be kept in pots of their own or they will take over the whole show.

Window boxes can be used either side of the glass. Again, they are excellent for herbs. Cover the soil with pebbles and it will take on the appearance of an oriental garden. If your window sill is not large enough to hold a box, you can buy special brackets that fix to the outside wall and support a box. Drainage trays are only needed for indoor boxes. Most garden centres have a large selection of different size boxes, the deeper the better for perennial plants.

Hanging baskets Everybody fills their hanging baskets with begonias and trailing lobelia. But why not try trailing tomatoes, runner beans or mint. Wire baskets need a peat liner (available from garden centres), or better still, lining with moss. Gather moss from trees, or anywhere moist like guttering or drainpipes. Old lawns often contain moss that can be raked out with a leaf rake. Gently firm the moss around the wire frame, the green parts facing outside as much as possible, fill with potting compost and water. Plastic hanging baskets need no lining. Remember when hanging your basket that it will weigh two or three times as much watered and planted up in midseason than when first prepared, so make sure your fixtures can take it.

Growbags You can either buy organic growbags (suppliers listed at the end of this book) or you can easily make your own. Take a heavy duty plastic bag and fill with potting compost. Tie up the end and lay on its side in a gravel tray or some other protective layer. If you are careful not to over-water, growbags are large enough to make drainage unnecessary. A 75cm (30in) bag will take two or three tomato plants. Simply cut three holes into the top of the bag, water, and plant out the tomatoes. Support tall plants with bamboo canes. Smaller plants, like lettuce, can go closer together. Growbags are the cheapest way to grow indoors and they create a garden wherever you want, growing anything from miniature lettuce to bush marrows.

TEN

Indestructible Vegetables

Indestructible vegetables are plants that will take almost any amount of abuse and neglect, but still bear a good crop. They are the perfect start for the indoor garden—a touch of Gaia on the window sill. What is more, they can be grown at practically any time of the year.

Baby greens

Here are some of the fastest growing greens you will ever come across and do not even need germinating. What some people throw away, we can turn into a source of wealth.

Beetroot (beet) is usually grown for its roots, but its leaves are delicious, especially young. The next time you buy raw beetroot from a shop, cut away the crown about 1cm (½in) from the top. Grate the beetroot into your favourite salad, but save the crown and plant it in a compost-filled pot with just the top showing. Water, and within a week the first new growth should start to show. Pick the leaves while they are still small, 7.5–15cm (3–6in) high, and use them in salads or lightly sautéed like spinach. The fresher the beetroot the better the growth, so choose well! Baby greens need little space, so crowd half a dozen tops into a larger pot and get a worthwhile crop.

Carrot greens have the same texture and taste as a cross between coriander and parsley. Grow the same way as the beetroot greens, but let the leaves get a little larger before harvesting. They make an attractive garnish to salads.

Garlic greens have a milder flavour than crushed cloves, last longer, and save all the bother of fiddling with the garlic press. They can be grown simply by pushing individual cloves 2.5cm (1in) apart into a compost-filled flower pot 12.5–15cm (5–6in) deep. Harvest the young shoots when they are 15–20cm (6–8in) high. Cut 3.5cm (1in) from their base and chop like spring onions or chives. The shoots will regrow several times.

Lentil greens   We have already sprouted lentils, but scattered on the

87

surface of a shallow tray covered with 2.5–4cm (1–1½in) of potting compost, they will root and produce young green shoots ready to eat in a week to ten days. Snip near the surface with a pair of scissors to harvest. They will regrow two or three times.

Mustard and cress greens, either grown individually or combined, have far more flavour than store-bought 'cress' which is really rape. Mustard greens are full of iron, calcium and vitamins A and C. Grow like lentil greens.

Shallots can be harvested early and used like spring onions (scallions) at a time of year when bunches would still be extortionately priced in the shops. Plant 5–6 bulbs close together in a pot 15cm (6in) deep, anytime between mid-winter and late spring, and watch them sprout up to eight green shoots each. When the shoots are 15–30cm (6–12in) high and it is easy to peel off the outer onion layers, pull them up as needed, remove the layers, wash and use as spring onions. Each bulb will produce the equivalent of one store-bought bunch of spring onions (scallions).

Turnip and Swede (rutabaga) tops are grown just like beetroot. You will find almost any green leaf is sweet if picked young enough.

Bon appetit! What other baby greens can you discover that will bring green life into you home?

ELEVEN

The Indoor Herb Garden

Herbs are low maintenance plants, many ideally suited to growing indoors, either in separate pots or in creative window box combinations. Hazel Evans suggests growing mint in hanging baskets; the roots soon poke through the basket frame, covering the basket in a carpet of fragrant green. Many herbs are perennial (they last for more than one year like trees and shrubs) which means you can continue to harvest all year round. A lettuce may be gone in a single meal, but herbs add fresh flavour to your meals every day of the week. I have listed ten useful and flavourful herbs that can be grown indoors. As usual, only grow what will delight and what you will use (although herbs make excellent presents, especially if you have grown them yourself). Do not waste your time and space with some species whose upkeep is nothing but a chore when you could be growing something really exciting.

Most herbs are inexpensive, and can be bought the size you want them. With careful harvesting/pruning you will be able to keep them that size. If you do not want to buy, there are three ways you can propagate herbs, depending on the variety and your own needs:

Sowing   Annuals like basil need sowing each year, perhaps twice to get a good winter supply. Most perennials can also be sown, but it's easier and quicker to use another propagation method. If temperature allows, you could sow any time of the year, but it is best to stay within a few weeks of outdoor sowing times, so the plant is growing fast when the sun is strong in the sky—even indoors, it is best to work with Nature's rhythms.

Division   Plants that are not hard wooded with a single main stem can be dug up, divided and repotted. Chives, comfrey, mint, marjoram, and lemon balm can all be propagated this way. Division also restores vigour to the old stock, so you can do your neighbours a favour by taking a clump of their chives. Cut lush growth back before repotting, especially with large leaved mints, and let them regrow.

Cuttings are simpler than most people think. Bay, lavender, rosemary, sage, winter savory, thyme and most woody shrubs will set from cuttings. The simplest way is to take *heel cuttings* from the parent plant: a 7.5–15cm (3–6in) side branch is broken off so that a large open area is exposed—the heel. Remove the bottom leaves, place the heel in a jar of water for a few weeks and let the new white roots grow. Pot out in a sunny place, and keep damp while the roots establish.

Heel cuttings

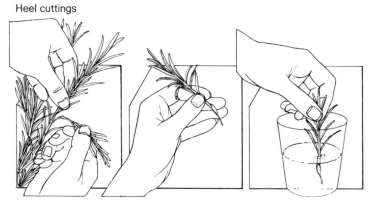

Break off cutting from   Remove bottom leaves   Place in water
parent plant

Perennial herbs in a window box or small pots need *repotting* each year into larger pots to stop them becoming too rootbound and replenish nutrients in the soil. Larger pots (over 30cm (12in) in diameter) and tubs only need repotting every few years.

Ten kitchen herbs

Basil is an annual plant. Sow with plenty of moisture and gentle heat in early spring, and perhaps again in late summer for winter cutting. Basil will not tolerate frost at all. First picking should come by midsummer, and continue until midwinter. Nip out the growing tip to keep the plants bushy. Bush and Greek Basil grow about 30cm (12in) high—a good size for indoors. Leslie, my mother, has 4 or 5 plants on a sunlit window sill near the kitchen door. One plant does not seem to cope with demand!
Bay is the exact opposite to basil. A doctor friend has two huge bay trees outside his front door, exposed to the ravages of London bustle,

and patients taking the odd leaf for their stew. Cuttings are the best method of propagating. Keep the cutting in a humid atmosphere, either in a propagator or with a plastic bag over the pot. After the first two years when bay should be kept out of frost, it will tolerate most temperatures, but give it enough light. Do not pick the leaves until the plant has enough to spare or you will slow growth. Finally, plant out in large pots or containers. You can dictate the size by careful pruning.

Chives are part of the onion family. Seeds only grow slowly, so get your chives from dividing someone else's clump, or buy from a nursery. Always keep enough green for the plant to grow back. In cold weather chives will die back into their small bulbs and regrow next year so keep their corner of the window box moist. Flowers resemble red clover; a beautiful garnish but they slow down leaf growth.

Mint comes in an amazing array of varieties, all precocious, and all easy to grow. Like lemon balm, keep mint to a pot of its own or the roots will quickly invade the space of other plants. Outdoors they quickly become weeds as persistent as couch grass, but behave themselves if the roots are contained by a pot, bricks, or other physical barriers from the rest of the garden. Peppermint, spearmint, Eau de Cologne mint, apple mint, pineapple mint, ginger mint . . . are just some of the varieties on offer, each with a different appearance, scent, and flavour. They may die back in winter, but you can bet your bottom dollar they will be back in spring. Cut back growth when dividing and repotting or the leaves will wilt. Keep moist, and spray with soapy water if aphids become a problem. Mint adds a wonderful cool flavour to summer fruit punches.

Parsley is not nearly as difficult to grow as people say. I have a strong affection for this crop because it's related to the carrot, and at one time I was growing some of the best parsley seen at Cardiff wholesale market. Sow the seeds very thinly in early spring. The long thin, carrot-like cotyledons will emerge about 14 days later. Harden the young plants outside if possible before finally potting them on indoors. The secret to parsley is to grow single plants spaced far apart. Parsley sown close together will yield nothing by stalk when you want large, dark green, heavily curled leaves. Start picking when the plant has growth to spare and regrowth will come fast. Moss curled is the most common English variety, but I think French parsley has more sophistication and flavour. Both are biennial (like carrots, they have a two year life cycle), and withstand most winters if cut back.

Pot marjoram, unlike sweet or knotted marjoram, stays green all winter, has smaller leaves, and stands more upright, reducing the space it needs to grow. It can be propagated from cuttings in spring or autumn, or sown in mid- to late spring. A good window box companion.

Rosemary can grow up to 180cm (6 feet) tall. A large plant in the hallway or living room will scent the house like few other plants can—it reminds me of hot summer days just after rain. I was sold a creeping rosemary from a herbary in St Davids, Pembrokeshire, for my herb window box which has worked very well, trailing over the side of the box next to the thyme. I keep it about 15cm (6in) tall by trimming excess growth. In a couple of years I will dig up the plant and re-root a cutting to keep the small size with lots of leaf. Take cuttings from late spring to midsummer, or sow the seed in mid-spring. Rosemary is a wonderful plant to live with.

Sage prefers drier soil, so plant it away from moisture-loving chives and basil. Its grey-green leaves make it easily recognizable. Dwarf sage is good for window boxes, but it is easy to keep any variety under control. You may like to try red, purple, golden, or silver sages. Take cuttings in midsummer, or sow seed mid-spring. A single plant should last you three years, but protect against severe frosts if it's outside. Left to its own devices all but the dwarf sage will grow about 45cm (18in).

Thyme is a herb from the seashore, at home in dry sandy soils and liquid seaweed feeding. No plant will grow more than 23cm (9in) high, and may hug the ground less than 7.5cm (3in) tall. It is small, but a little goes a long way preparing salads, steamed vegetables, soups and meat dishes. Take cuttings in midsummer. Thyme does not like acid soils, from peat-based composts, so add a little calcified seaweed or crushed eggshells to restore the pH.

Winter savory is a perennial shrub with some of the same flavour of sage. It is not the same plant as summer savory which is an annual. Like sage, it likes drier, sandy soil, especially in winter. The seed is slow to germinate, so take cuttings in midsummer. Plants will grow 30cm (12in) high, but can be cut back to 15cm (6in) in winter. The cuttings can be dried and used to flavour fish or in savoury butter. Savory takes its name from those mythological beasts, Satyrs, with whom it has long been associated. It will survive all but the hardest frosts and grows by spreading its branches outwards with vertical shoots which flower purple/pink flowers in midsummer.

TWELVE

More Indoor Wonders

What other vegetables can we grow indoors? We need plants that will suit each of the different micro-climates of our own homes—everything from the outside window box to the greenhouse environment of the conservatory. Here are a few suggestions of plants which thrive in hanging baskets, are seductive in window boxes, and turn tubs into fountains of organic splendour.

Beetroot (beet) is an indoor winner because it will tolerate cool conditions and you can eat both the tops and the roots. Sow a bolt resistant variety like Bolthardy (so you do not have to worry about spring cold spells), from early spring through to mid-summer. The seeds are large—each husk is actually a cluster of seeds that may produce more than one plant—and can easily be sown individually in 10cm (4in) pots with good moisture. Prick out unwanted seedlings. Alternatively, sow three seeds together, spaced 25cm (10in) apart, in growbags or 25cm (10in) pots. When the seeds germinate, leave the best five or six seedlings to grow on as a bunch—the leaves will grow up to 30cm (12in) high. Like so many of our vegetables, beetroot comes from the seashore, and appreciates a regular foliar feed of liquid seaweed. It collects iodine which helps protect against radiation and cancer of the thyroid.

Chicories are the new wonders to small space gardens. They and their close partners, endive, come in a seductive mixture of colours from the most intense green to blood red, and of vastly different shapes and sizes. Their hardiness is one of their great benefits, which makes them ideal winter salad vegetables.

Witloof chicory is the most common and is the normal forcing chicory. (See The Outdoor Garden, for further details.)

Green cutting chicories are fast growing varieties that can be harvested when their leaves are only 5–7.5cm (2–3in) high. Spadona is the variety I have tried indoors, broadcast into a 40cm (16in) saucer, 7.5cm (3in) deep. Keep the soil moist with a plastic bag or sheet of glass on top to ensure even germination. These chicories are harvested on a cut-and-come-again basis, but if you want a good succession of crops, choose a deeper container—at least 15cm (6in) deep. Harvest with scissors or a sharp knife close to ground level. Fast growth means the plants are hungry for nitrogen, either in rich potting compost or a liquid feed. Sow anytime between early spring and late summer, either in succession, or once for a permanent chicory bed that will last you the entire season. There are many other varieties that can be grown this way, including Sugar Loaf if it is broadcast.

Courgettes (zucchini) are great to grow because of the sheer volume each plant produces. Grow space saving bush plants instead of the trailing varieties, although even these can reach 180cm (6 feet) in length by the end of summer—not really the plant for the kitchen windowsill, but they are spectacular flowing out of a large 35–50cm (14–20in) diameter hanging basket, or from a balcony tub. After the fruit has set, the flowers make a wonderful garnish to salads, or an unusual starter lightly sautéed with cashew nuts.

Courgettes are really immature marrows, but now new varieties are bred especially for their production. Try one of the F1 hybrids which are usually earlier and yield more. *Early Gem* produces early dark green courgettes, *Zucchini* a mottled-green fruit, and *Burpee Golden Zucchini* long, golden fruit.

Sow individually in 8.5cm (3½in) pots in late spring for the earliest crops. They will germinate easily and grow fast in warm conditions. Keep the soil watered and give them plenty of light so they produce large leaves instead of long stems. Plant out into 30cm (12in) pots, large hanging baskets, or tubs or plant 45cm (18in) apart into growbags. They will prefer hot, humid conservatory conditions, but will grow well anywhere after the last risk of frost has passed. The only thing they do not like is wind as it may damage their rather brittle stems. Do not let them wilt because it slows down cropping—you cannot really overwater courgettes. A good mulch of pebbles, leaves, moss or straw will go a long way to keeping the soil wet. A rich compost, full of organic matter in any form, will help retain moisture and keep them fed. Pick the fruit as soon as it is ready as this stimulates the plant to produce more—with luck you can keep cropping until early autumn. There are no real pest problems, all they need is enough light and space to grow. If you can give them both they will bring a tropical feel to your home.

Lettuce   Achieve the best results from your space either by broad-casting or by using the new dwarf lettuce varieties.

The most common dwarf varieties are *Little Gem*, a small semi-cos, very sweet which also keeps well, and *Tom Thumb*, a butterhead type, five of which will fit into one 30cm (12in) pot. (Sow the seed either in a seedtray and prick out, or directly into their final growing positions.) Some butterheads will not germinate in high summer temperatures, so avoid excess heat. Plant out as soon as possible. Indoor lettuce will have larger, finer leaves than the same plant grown outdoors, which makes them tender, but also more vulnerable to disease and wilting in direct sunlight. Do not let lettuce dry out–once they are used to watering, they will expect it every day. Sow a few seeds frequently, especially in summer, to achieve continuity of supply.

'Salad Bowl' types of lettuce do not form tight compact hearts. They are harvested either by removing individual leaves from each plant like parsley, or cutting the leaves near the base and allowing them to regrow two or three times. Many of the varieties are unfamiliar in Britain and, except for *Salad Bowl* itself, other varieties will only be found in specialist seed catalogues. One way around this is to use a common variety like *Hilde*, *Avoncrisp*, and *Avondefiance* planted close together or broadcast. More unusual varieties include: *Green Australian Curled*, *Red American Curled* and *Red Italian* cutting lettuce, for which there are many names. Either sow in a seedtray and prick out to about 5cm (2in) apart in all directions, or broadcast very thinly to get the same rough spacing. Harvest whichever way you wish. If plants are closer than 5cm (2in) I suggest the cut-and-come-again method, rather than trying to select leaves from each plant. I often sow the seeds thicker than suggested and harvest with scissors— regrowth is always very fast, especially with a good foliar feed.

Lettuce are liable to bolt (run to seed) in hot weather; butterhead varieties are the worst. Prevent this by frequent sowings so that your lettuce do not sit waiting to be eaten. Botrytis can also cause trouble, especially in stagnant, cold conditions, and aphids may make washing the leaves a real chore. If you have any trouble turn to the Banishing Pests chapter.

Carrots—my favourite! Use a short rooted variety like *Early Nantes*, or the funny-looking round rooted varieties like *Rondo* that, apart from the colour, look more like beetroot. Sow the seed any time of the year in their permanent location—carrots will not stand transplanting.

Aim for a 5–7.5cm (2–3in) spacing between plants, in rows 15cm (6in) apart. Do not thin as this attracts the dreaded carrot root fly. Bring a little romance into your home by sowing carrots around the rim of your tomato containers, (carrots love tomatoes), or interspace your rows with garlic.

The seed is slow to germinate—about 14 days—and the first signs of life (besides the weeds) will be two tiny thin cotyledons. These will eventually grow into strong, crunchy, red-rooted carrots. Grown indoors their tops will reach a stringy 45cm (18in) in height. This is normal in warmer conditions, so do not worry as long as they are getting enough light. Early spring, and autumn sowings need a hardy variety like *Early Nantes*, or *Amsterdam Forcing*. A later summer sowing should give you carrots by mid-winter. Carrot root fly is a pest—see chapter 18 for details.

Radish can be ready eight weeks from sowing, which makes them one of the fastest crops to grow. Picked young, organic radish are a very different vegetable from the hot, woody, store-bought monsters. These are sweet and succulent. *French Breakfast* is the usual variety. Sow 4cm (1½in) apart in rows 10cm (4in) apart, or along tub and flower pot borders amongst the parsley and garlic. The first leaves will be up in 72 hours. Harvest as soon as the scarlet globe is worth eating. And do not forget the leaves as well, chopped finely in a salad.

Runner beans look fantastic interwoven with sweet peas around the bars of a balcony or outside staircase. Soak the seeds overnight and sow initially into 7.5cm (3in) pots in late spring. Grow indoors until the frost has passed and plant out into tubs, growbags, or hanging baskets in late spring–early summer. (Alternatively sow outside directly at the end of spring.) *Achievement*, *Enorma* and *Prizewinner* are all tall (or long if you are trailing them), heavy yielding varieties. Two plants per square foot should give the highest yields. Sow your sweet peas the same way. Their coloured flowers will complement the red flower of the bean. Start harvesting in mid-summer when beans are 15–20cm (6–8in) long. Freeze what you cannot eat. In late summer, let the last pods fill and mature, and harvest the seed for next year, (as long as you have not used a hybrid variety whose seeds will not be of the same genetic makeup as the parent plant).

Spring onions (scallions) are better grown in clumps like chives than sown in a row. Start with gentle heat for spring and autumn sowings. An 8.5cm (3½in) pot will take about 15 seeds. Keep the soil moist during germination and early growth. *White Lisbon* is the main variety. I sow spring onions for use after my shallots have finished. They need good, nitrogen-rich soil for strong growth, and respond well to heat. As they start to grow away, give them less water—spring onions, like all their relatives, are used to a dry environment and suffer from mildew if conditions are too wet. Harvest when your crop is 15–20cm (6–8in) tall.

Tomatoes are not just the salad tomatoes you buy in the shops, picked green and artificially ripened. You can grow small, sweet cherry tomatoes, or the fat juicy Italian giants, plum, or marmalade tomatoes. The choice is yours. I am going to concentrate on salad tomatoes and cherry tomatoes from bush plants.

Sow salad tomatoes in late winter/early spring in gentle heat. There are many varieties. I have used *Curato* and *Alicante*. Only *Moneymaker* I would not use because it is a rather flavourless variety. Prick the seedlings out into 8.5cm (3½in) pots—peat pots if you have them—and keep them in a warm position. It will take about eight weeks between sowing and final planting out into 25–30cm (10–12in) pots, when the seedlings have grown to about 20–30cm (8–12in) tall and are starting to form their first truss (stem of 6 to 8 flowers). Growbags are an excellent alternative, with tomato plants spaced 30cm (12in) apart (about three plants to a bag). Do not feed the plants before you plant them out. You will get a heavier crop if the plants are slightly starved so they look drawn and anaemic; the stress induces them to produce fruit instead of leaf growth.

Place in a warm sunny position. Tomatoes are only half hardy, and indoor varieties need heat to grow. Prick out any side shoots that will form where the leaves meet the stem (*not* the trusses that hold the flowers). Pinch out the growing tip when the fifth truss has formed; the plant should be 150–180cm (5–6 feet) tall. Support with bamboo canes or string hung from the ceiling and gently spiralled round the stem. As the flowers open, give them a little flick with your finger to make sure they have been pollinated and the fruit will set.

As soon as the first truss starts to set, start feeding with liquid seaweed, sprayed with a hand sprayer over the leaves every few days. Keep plants well watered, especially on hot days. A mulch goes a long way to retain moisture. You will know if your plants are nourished because the new leaves will unfold from tight crinkly balls, rather like a fern. (This is also true for potatoes, which are the same family.)

Leave the first ripe fruit on the plant until others ripen—the presence of one seems to induce others to follow suit. At the end of summer, harvest all remaining unripened tomatoes to use as chutney, or ripen off the plant on the kitchen shelf.

Bush varieties give better value for space, and have been bred for outdoors, though their success largely depends on the kind of summer. No tomato plant will tolerate frost, which means they cannot be planted outdoors until late spring, but at the same time they need long summer days of heat if they are to ripen. That is why I think they are well suited for the indoor garden. *Pixie*, *Red Alert*, and *Sleaford Abundance* are all excellent candidates for hanging baskets or tubs, either indoors or on the balcony or patio. Dwarf varieties like *Pixie* or *Small Fry* will squeeze into window boxes or 20cm (8in) pots.

Follow the same methods as above, but harden off carefully before setting plants outside—any sudden blast of cold may check their growth. Bush varieties do not need staking and are happy to hang over the side of a hanging basket or tub where their red fruit make a startling display. There is no need to prick out side shoots or the growing tip as the plants are naturally self regulating. If you are growing outdoors, choose a sunny aspect, space plants 60cm (24in) apart, and put straw or some other insulator between them and the damp ground to prevent them rotting and to keep slugs off. The trusses will be full of small bite-size tomatoes, much sweeter than other varieties. You can easily buy both bush or salad tomato plants in late spring, but be careful you know which variety you are getting.

Like potatoes, tomatoes are susceptible to blight. Bronzed foliage, with small mite underneath is the sign of red spider mite, (see chapter 19 on banishing pests for details). Sticky black moulds on leaves and white dart-shaped insects are whitefly but these can be overcome by planting marigolds or nasturtium nearby.

II   THE OUTDOOR GARDEN

From one small patch of green, more vegetables than you ever imagined

Outdoors the adventure rolls on. The methods outlined in this section are part of a new understanding of what it is to work with Nature. They do not signal the return to subsistence agriculture, scraping an existence from the land, but the integration of small space gardening into our daily lives as a means of creating the wealth of the 80's. New insight has come from the mistakes we have made in the destruction of Gaia, our diminished health, and outmoded ideas of how to get rich. *The Outdoor Garden* is nothing more than planting this new understanding in Earth. What have we found?

THIRTEEN

The Five Loves of Gaia

Gaia's first love is life

Life creates life, sustains life, and increases life. Organic gardening maximizes the biological life of the soil, creating high vitality plants, free from deficiencies and disease, high in structural information and essential nutrients that make our own high health possible. Gaia is unique in the entire known universe as the only planet that is not part of the great entropic decay of all matter. Only Gaia builds order instead of grinding it down the way rain levels a mountain. Chemical fertilizers and pesticides do not feed life. They destroy it, work against Gaia, and the creatures that inhabit her surface.

Gaia's second love is variety

She is nothing if not gregarious. Like a good party, the more the merrier. More soil bacteria, more worms and, on the surface, more plant varieties through rotation, intercropping, succession planting and companion planting—all essential ingredients for modern organic methods. Monoculture is a symptom of disease. If one weed predominates in your garden, it's a sign that something is wrong. There is nothing exclusive about Gaia—the wealth of any aspect increases the wealth of all.

Ground cover is Gaia's third love

She hates being exposed to the sun, wind and rain that break down her soil and leech away her nutrients. Ground that cannot cover itself is dead. Nature's emergency cover is weeds. We can improve on this through extensive use of mulches, new spacing methods, and green manure crops.

Gaia's fourth love is continuity

She thinks in cycles, not in straight lines which always have a beginning and an end. Chemical growing exalts linear thinking in terms of input-output because it believes this is the way to wealth. But Gaia's power lies in her cycles, from the vast homeostatic feedback mechanisms that maintain the precise conditions for life on Earth, to the nutrient cycles of your compost bin.

Gaia's final love is man

At times he is a parasite on her flesh. But at his best, when he is not intimidated by change, or frightened by success, he is Gaia's best companion. She loves to work with him because he has the ability to bring out the best in her. The soils of Britain and Northwest Europe are man's creation over thousands of years of cultivation. Man has drained land where there was only swamp, and built up soil fertility through the cultivated use of animals and crop rotation. Without man's constant attention, many of Europe's soils would quickly turn into acid and waterlogged wastelands where earthworms and many bacteria could not survive. You can see the strength of Europe's soils by the beating they take with modern farming methods. The virgin soils of North America have none of this cultivated strength and their life can now be counted in years rather than decades if we do not change. Man can help Gaia realize her full potential. We have made mistakes, and even the most experienced organic gardener has crop failures and upsets the biological balance once in a while. If we do not make mistakes we do not learn, which makes me think the most important question is one of having our hearts in the right place. The good husbandry of the Earth has always been a love affair between Gaia and man.

FOURTEEN

What Are Your Resources?

What you grow, how much, and how often will depend on the resources available. It is pointless raising 500 cabbage plants if you can cross your garden in two strides, or sowing carrots in autumn if they are going to spend the first six months of their life under snow. We will get the most out of our garden, and have pleasure doing it if we first see what we have got to work with.

Here are some resources worth considering:

Garden size   How much space do you have available to grow vegetables? One square yard, or half an acre? It is better to garden a small space well than struggle with too much. After all, you can always expand if you are having fun, and mistakes are better made on a small scale. I once lost 10,000 cabbage before I learnt about pigeons—I wish I had learnt with half a dozen.

Soil   Have you got any? Or is your garden a mass of rubble left by the builders? Be realistic about what you have, then we will build. No site is so barren that Gaia cannot reclaim it as her own.

A pile of rubble can be transformed into a productive garden only with large quantities of organic matter. Try to get hold of stable or cow manure, leaves, or peat. If possible, dig the manure into the soil, and add an extra 15–30cm (6–12in) on top. Even if you're lucky enough to have soil in your garden, organic matter on heavy clays will improve drainage, bring air into the ground, warm it and make it a fit habitat for soil oranisms and worms. On the other hand, if you have a light, sandy soil, organic matter will improve its water holding qualities and structure, preventing it from drying out in summer and 'capping' after rain.

Climate   Is your growing season cut short each year by the environmental disaster we call winter, or can you step outside and pick oranges off the trees on Christmas Day? Water, temperature and sunlight are the main limiting factors to most plant growth. In the cool, temperate climates of Northwest Europe, much of North

America, and parts of Australia, we can increase temperature with the use of cloches, indoor germination, and other methods of crop protection. Hotter, Mediterranean and sub-tropical climates need to conserve water and protect crops from too much sun with the use of mulches, and intercropping. For instance, sunflowers create excellent shade for the courgettes (zucchini) or pumpkins if they are planted together.

If you live in a warm climate, you will have to be careful of the organic matter in your soil, because your soil organisms will be working so fast they may well consume more organic material than you can hope to provide. Nature has overcome this problem in hot climates by 'locking up' almost all her nutrients in plant growth, keeping very little reserve in the soil. We can imitate Nature by never leaving our soil exposed to the elements and by sowing 'green manure' crops whenever possible (see p. 111). Compost should be spread when only half decomposed, and heavy mulches will help cool the soil and prevent water loss. One of the great British organic pioneers, Sir Albert Howard, did much of his research on organic systems in sub-tropical India, and I recommend his books to anyone who needs to maintain soil fertilitiy in hot climates.

Most vegetables listed in the Outdoor Garden are suited to temperate climates. If you are lucky enough to see the sun more often, you can grow plants we can only dream of in these cooler parts of the world, although the basic principles of Gaiaculture remain the same. In Britain, the north of the country is at least two weeks behind the south.

But wherever in the world you live, local climate is just as important to what you can grow, especially frost sensitive crops and those that need a long season. Frost pockets, height above sea level and exposure to the wind all affect what you can grow. Cities are generally a few degrees warmer than the country, but do the buildings in your street act as a wind tunnel? I live by the sea and lift my new potatoes while friends are planting theirs just 30 miles away in the hills. Look around and talk to neighbours to find out what grows well where you are.

Aspect The sun rises in the east and sets in the west. As it crosses the sky it will create shadows at different times of the day for different lengths of time. Watch the shadows move across your own garden. Which parts are in sun most of the day, and which only see shade?

Gently sloping, south-facing aspects will receive the most sun, and gardens sloping north the least. This can cut the amount of sunlight reaching your plants by over 50%, so try and maximize your garden area under the sun.

Water taps need to be in easy reach of your garden. Few things are more frustrating than having to walk into the bathroom to fill up the watering can, not to mention the state of the carpet when you have finished. It is well worth buying some black alkathene piping and running it to an outside standpipe from the kitchen plumbing.

It's organization like this that makes organic gardening a pleasure instead of a labour. What other logistics can you think of that will make your love affair with Gaia a long and happy one? How close are the compost bins to the kitchen door? Do you keep your gardening tools in the loft? Would a few paving stones help stop the garden path becoming a swamp after rain? Give yourself the best possible conditions—both you and your garden deserve it!

Time The length of time you spend in the garden is no measure of the satisfaction it will give you, the Earth, or even the amount of crops you grow. Many crops, like onions, potatoes, or swiss chard need very little attention. Early beetroot (beet) and spring onions (scallions) need more. Be honest about what you can *easily* afford to do, and plan your crops around that. After a while, your work with Gaia will fit naturally into the rhythm of your life, and as you discover the special qualities of your own garden and the different crops, you will find time is not as important as your skill of doing the right thing at the right time. This comes with practice.

Money, like time, is no indication of the wealth you can create in your garden. Fukuoka, the Japanese author of *The One Straw Revolution*, achieves higher continuous crops of rice and barley than the best chemical farmers in his country without the massive bankloans they thought they needed to buy sophisticated ploughing, harvesting and spray equipment. We can be shrewd about how we create our organic wealth.

FIFTEEN

Sowing Your Seed

'The crop is in the seedbed', said Pembrokeshire farmer Fred Mathias, as he surveyed the concrete desert where I had sown my carrot seeds. How I expected those tiny seeds to grow in such a wilderness, I do not know. Luckily, Fred showed me how to create the deep fine tilth I needed to give my crops the best possible start to life.

A fine tilth is what you need

Whether you are broadcasting your seed, station planting, or sowing in rows, you need the same fine tilth—the smaller the seed, the finer the tilth has to be. But what does a fine tilth look and feel like? Frost creates the best tilth. Pick up a piece of earth that has been exposed to a hard frost. It will crumble into super-fine granules in your hand. Or feel the castings of a molehill—this soil is so well prepared that gardeners use it as potting compost.

A fine tilth also relies on plenty of organic material to retain its basic structure through soil crumbs. Without organic matter you can get a fine soil, but it will not hold its structure and the surface will 'cap', making a hard layer inpenetrable to your seedlings.

In order to prepare a seedbed in ground that has already been forked over and is not too wet, lightly fork the surface and rake smooth. Remove any large stones or leftover vegetation from weeding or the last crop. It is now ready for sowing. We have already talked about *planting out* and *station planting* in the Indoor Garden. For more information see the Spacesavers chapter. Let us concentrate here on *sowing in rows* (sometimes rows are called 'drills'), and the *broadcast method*.

Sowing in rows

Mark out your row in the seedbed with a line. Spacing depends on the crop and the size you want for each plant. With the wrong end of a hoe, or a dibbler, make a shallow drill along the length of the line, the depth of which also depends on the seed, but should be between 1–2cm (½–¾in) for most small seed. Sow the seed *as close to the final plant density as possible*. For instance, maincrop carrots want about 12 plants per 30cm (12in). If you can manage to sow say 15 seeds per 30cm (12in) to account for any losses, you will not waste time later thinning which encourages carrot root fly. (I never thin if I can help it.) Then gently return the soil on top of the seeds with your hand. I sometimes mark the row with a light sprinkling of sand along the line, but this is not essential as long as you have markers at each end of the drill, one with details of the variety and date sown. Remove the line and firm the row with your hand or feet. Water in the evening if the ground is dry.

As soon as the seedlings are large enough to be seen, weed, even if there are only a few weeds in sight. If you use a hoe, the action will create a 'dust mulch' in hot weather that will help prevent water loss and the ground cracking.

Seeds, like carrots, beetroots (beet) and leaf beets, peas, broad beans (fava beans) and spinach, can also be scattered in drills 5cm (2in) wide which gives you a much higher concentration of plants (for example, about 20 carrots per 30cm (12in) instead of twelve). The advantages of this are that plants often appreciate the protection offered by numbers, they are less prone to be flattened by the wind, and especially tall plants like peas and broad beans gain through mutual support. Yields per foot can also be higher, although weeding amongst the rows will have to be done by hand.

Broadcast sowing tips

Cut-and-come-again lettuce, Italian chicories and other exotic salad crops can be sown broadcast method. The seeds are small and need the best seedbed you can offer. Prepare the seedbed as before, and scatter the seeds over the surface. Gently rake over to cover them, and firm down with your hand or foot.

You will get best results if you broadcast in an area with few weeds, as it is difficult to distinguish between crop and weed in the early stages of growth. You will also help germination if you give a light watering in the evening and then cover with a piece of black plastic, newspaper, or best of all, a damp hessian sack. This will help to prevent the soil from drying out. Remove as soon as the plants begin to appear.

SIXTEEN

Organic Fertilizers

Plants need light, air, water and certain elements to grow. The three main elements are Nitrogen, Phosphorus, and Potash (commonly known as NPK), but many trace elements are also essential for strong healthy growth. Organic fertilizers are natural products made available to plants through the life of the soil. But nutrients like N, P and K and the trace elements are not enough—*soil structure* is a vital ingredient in the maintenance of soil health. Some organic fertilizers provide both nutrients and soil structure. Others, particularly bought-in mineral- and animal-based fertilizers, do not—an important consideration when we start to think about how to feed our soil. The chart below gives an indication of which organic fertilizers can provide us with these needs.

WHAT CAN ORGANIC FERTILIZERS PROVIDE?

Fertilizer:	*Garden made*	*Build soil structure*	*Provide nutrients*
Garden compost:	YES	YES	YES
Potting compost:	NO	NO	YES
Green manures:	YES	YES	YES
Animal manures:	NO	YES	YES
Mineral & animal fertilizers:	NO	NO	YES
Seaweed (fresh & meal):	NO	YES	YES
Seaweed (calcified & liquid):	NO	NO	YES

This chapter explains in more detail the benefits of each of these ways of feeding the soil and begins with the amazing qualities of the compost heap.

The incredible heap—how to make your own compost

The compost heap breaks down organic waste in a controlled way, so that the maximum amount of nutrients return to the soil. A good heap can have 28% *more nitrogen* when it is finished than at the start, through the help of nitrogen-fixing bacteria. But, like brewing beer or any other biological process, compost making is an art. We will look at the guidelines here, but it is practice that will make you an expert.

The compost heap and rubbish heap are not the same thing. The compost heap is a specially designed 5-star hotel for select bacteria which create priceless sweet smelling, dark, water retentive, nutrient rich compost in a matter of weeks. These VIPs need air, moisture, insulation from the cold and a varied and plentiful supply or organic matter. How can we meet these needs?

There are many designs for compost bins. Any one will do, as long as it is about 90cm (3 feet) in all directions (to provide sufficient insulation for bacteria), has a lid, and ventilation holes to give the bacteria air. You can buy the small 'dustbin' type bins from garden centres—just make sure it is strong enough to stand constant use and come up to the 5-star standards of our bacteria. Whatever design you choose, put it on well drained soil that is easy to reach without a combat jacket and grappling hook, but not on your prime growing space. If you choose the other end of the garden, lay a path to the kitchen door so that emptying the kitchen compost bucket does not turn into a major expedition. If you build it on grass, turn the turf first, as this will prevent the bottom layer becoming acid and help the free movement of worms. Heavy soils benefit from a layer of rubble, or a few bricks to help drainage and ventilation.

When the bin is full, wait until the centre has heated up. Then turn the heap so the outside now becomes the centre, and wait for the heating up process to happen again. (This gives the whole heap a chance to go through the decomposition process.) A good heap can be ready to use in 6 weeks during summer, but may take 6 months in winter. It is ready when it has cooled and is full of red nematode worms. The compost should be sweet smelling, spongy and rich textured, without any signs of the banana peels and lawn mowings that originally went in. Sieve your compost through 2.5cm (1in) squares before spreading on the garden, and return to the bin any elements that have not fully decomposed.

What makes a 5-star compost bin?

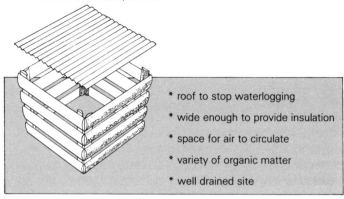

* roof to stop waterlogging
* wide enough to provide insulation
* space for air to circulate
* variety of organic matter
* well drained site

What goes into a heap?

Practically anything that has once lived and will easily decompose is fit composting material. Collect kitchen waste in your compost bucket under the sink, lined with a plastic bag or a few sheets of newspaper that can be tipped on the heap with their contents. The bucket can be filled with:

★ vegetable trimmings and waste
★ coffee grounds and tea leaves (delicacies in the compost world)
★ banana and other fruit peel
★ up to 10% newspaper if it is shredded first (but not glossy paper)
★ ash from wood fires (but not soot)
★ eggshells

(Avoid cooked food as it may attract rats, or large bones because they take too long to decompose.)

Garden offerings to the compost heap can include:

★ weeds—especially in a good heap where heat will destroy the seeds
★ spent potting compost
★ small hedge trimmings
★ leaves
★ lawn cuttings

(Large branches will not decompose, and it is best to break up woody plant tissue like cabbage and sunflower stalks first with a hammer before throwing them in.)

Other material includes practically anything organic that you can beg or steal. Town gardeners can add volumes to their heap this way—it just takes a bit of ingenuity. For instance:

★ greengrocers throw away boxes of rotting compost delicacies each day and leaves are collected by the local council each autumn and dumped
★ straw can be added up to 50% of volume
★ animal manure is a compost activator
★ roadside mowings (as long as the road is not too busy with the risk of lead)
★ green bracken (ferns) contains 2.75% potash
★ seaweed
★ sawdust

(Go easy on the sawdust, or wood chippings, as they could rob nitrogen from your heap. Leaves in any quantity are better used on their own as a mulch than in a heap where they are rather wasted.)

How to build a heap

The secret of a 5-star heap is *variety*. A solid layer of lawn mowings lacks structure and will compact into an anaerobic (airless) fermenting mess. But mixed with straw, leaves, or old plant stalks, they will breakdown sweetly. Kitchen waste, greengrocer rejects and animal manure, also tend to have a high water content, so mix them with drier, more fibrous ingredients.

Build your heap in layers, never letting one material dominate. This is sometimes difficult in summer when the grass grows like wildfire, or a friend suddenly delivers a load of horse manure, but it is better to delay adding these treasures until you have found other ingredients to complement them than to destroy the first class environment in your bin.

If your soil tends to be acid you can sprinkle a handful of calcified seaweed on every 15–23cm (6–9in) of heap as you build.

Potting composts

Potting composts are not the same as the compost that comes from your heap, although many gardeners used sieved compost as part of their own unique potting compost recipe. Potting composts are specially formulated mixtures devised to give indoor sown seeds the best possible start in life (even if they are later going to be transplanted outside, like early lettuce). In order to achieve this, they are mixed to drain well but not dry out, have a texture fine enough for small seeds and enough nutrients to promote fast, healthy growth.

There are a number of commercial organic potting composts on the market—see back of book for suppliers. On the other hand, if your garden is large enough, you may like to mix your own. Herb grower Bernie Stevens let me have this excellent recipe from his herbary in St Davids, Pembrokeshire, which I have slightly modified:

2 parts peat
2 parts sterilized soil or compost
1 part coarse builders sand, or silver sand
50g (2oz) fish, blood and bone or fishmeal per 9 litres (2 gallons) of mixture
50g (2oz) of seaweed meal per 9 litres (2 gallons) of mixture
225g (8oz) of calcified seaweed per 9 litres (2 gallons) of mixture

A normal bucket holds 9 litres (2 gallons) by volume, and a handful of fertilizer weighs about 50g (2oz). Mix the recipe together in a wheelbarrow and use immediately, or keep for a few months in a heavy duty plastic bag out of the rain. The same mixture has a variety of uses:

1 as a seed compost in the seedtray during initial germination,
2 a compost for potting plants on before planting out,
3 a compost for long term growth in pots, containers, tubs, hanging baskets, and growbags.

Green manures

Nature creates soil fertility through plant growth. We can imitate Nature with green manures—crops grown for their fertility benefits that are dug back into the ground rather than harvested. They make excellent companions to barrowloads of animal manure if you are just starting to reclaim poor, low fertility soil. Different green manures bring different benefits to the soil. Some can even be sown in autumn so that they do not take up valuable cropping space during spring and summer. These benefits include:

Ground cover which suppresses weeds and locks up soil nutrients in plant growth instead of being leeched through the soil. This is especially important during winter, when rains can break down soil structure and wash away nutrients needed for next spring's crop.

Soil structure and humus formation is improved through the root systems of the green manures. They help create a stable, open soil structure, especially with the fibrous root systems of rye and clover. With green manures, you are making your own organic matter. Dug in, this green bulk helps increase the biological activity of the soil, releases plant nutrients and forms valuable humus.

Nitrogen fixing bacteria live in symbiotic relationship with all legumes (clovers, tares, vetches, lupins, peas and beans) which take nitrogen from the atmosphere, and make it available to plants. Sown in winter, these crops can increase the nitrogen in your soil, instead of letting rain wash it away. Lupins also provide phosphorus fixing fungi which extend from their roots.

Mineral gathering from the subsoil with long rooted manures like grazing rye, that becomes available when the crop is dug in.

Green manure crops include:

Annual lupins which are both nitrogen and phosphorus fixing. Sow 2.5cm (1in) deep, 15cm (6in) apart with 30cm (12in) between rows between mid-spring and midsummer. Dig in before it flowers, or cut down early crop and plant winter brassica into undug soil. Lupins take 8 weeks between sowing and maturity, 30g (1oz) will sow a 60m (200 feet) row.

Winter tares produce nitrogen, dense foliage, and can be sown in mid- to late summer after the last of the summer harvest. Sow 1cm (½ in) deep, 7.5cm (3in) apart, with 15cm (6in) between rows, or broadcast and rake in 30g (1oz) will sow a 24m (80 feet) row, or 30g (1oz) will broadcast a square metre/yard.

Grazing rye is very fast growing with a dense, fibrous mat of roots. Broadcast 30g (1oz) per square metre/yard anytime until late summer, and rake in. The rye will be up in ten days and will grow through the winter. Dig in before stalks start to form next spring. Very good for soil structure, does not fix nitrogen. Requires careful digging in to kill it in spring.

Mustard is fast growing and easily killed by frost. Use agricultural mustard, not the same seed as the mustard used for sprouting.

Broadcast 30g (1oz) per square metre/yard and rake in any time until later summer. Mustard is one of the most effective cures for wireworm—sharp orange larvae that eat rootcrops, especially in soil that has recently been lawn or pasture—but suffers from the drawback that it belongs to the same family as cabbage and can spread clubroot, so do not sow where cabbage are due in the next three years.

Animal manures

Animal manures boost soil structure and provide nutrients at the same time. The following table from Lawrence D. Hills' book *Organic Gardening* shows there is a good balance between all three major elements in all manures, which makes them a 'complete fertilizer', although high nitrogen manures can 'burn' plants and need to be applied in moderation. It is sometimes easy to forget that we are not feeding pigs but microscopic soil organisms, for whom a handful per square metre/yard is a feast.

PERCENTAGE OF NPK IN DIFFERENT ANIMAL MANURES

	nitrogen %	phosphate %	potash %
Horse	0.7	0.3	0.6
Cow	0.6	0.2	0.5
Pig	0.5	0.3	0.5
Sheep	0.7	0.3	0.4
Goat	1.44	0.2	1.0
Chicken	1.1	0.8	0.5
Rabbit	2.4	1.4	0.6
Pigeon	5.84	2.1	1.77

Animal manures also help restore barren or exhausted soils. If you are just converting a wasteland into your earthly paradise, apply cow or horse manure at least 15cm (6in) deep, dig it in, and grow a hardy crop like potatoes or broad beans. That will help soil fertility and structure recover.

Not all crops enjoy manure. Root crops tend to fork and produce too much top growth, so work your dressings into your rotation, for instance in spring before potatoes, cabbage, or peas.

Town and city dwellers may have trouble finding a supply of fresh manure, but many can now be bought in dried form, although they do not bring the same benefits to soil structure. But before you buy, check the label to make sure it's 100% organic.

Mineral and animal based fertilizers

We can also buy in organic nutrients to boost plant growth, but unlike fresh animal manures, garden compost or green manures, these fertilizers will not help maintain soil structure, and so are no substitute for these other fertility building methods. In general, blood and fish meal supply nitrogen needed for green growth. Bonemeal and rock phosphate provide phosphate needed for good fruit formation. Rock potash, seaweed and, to some extent, wood ashes contain potash, which is needed for strong stems, roots and disease resistance. Broken down into individual elements, these fertilizers provide the following:

Rock phosphate Ground rock with phosphate deposits. Slow acting unless ground to powder. Mined in Gafsa, Tunisia.
Analysis: P 28%
Rock potash A valuable source of potash
Analysis: K 11%
(Rock phosphate, and rock potash can be applied about 225g (8oz) per square metre/yard every couple of years.)
Bonemeal A useful supply of slow-releasing calcium and phosphate.
Analysis: N 4%, P 20%, Ca 60%
Available from most garden centres.
Dried blood Maybe the fastest releasing organic fertilizer. Won't burn lettuce plants like chemical counterparts. It is really a tonic rather than a fertilizer as it quickly disappears once applied to the soil.
Analysis: N 13%
Available from garden centres.
Fish meal Fast acting fertilizer, with nitrogen, phosphate and calcium, but no potash. Check the label to make sure potash has not been added chemically.
Analysis: N 7%, P 6%, Ca 16%.
Fish, blood and bone Again, a good supply of nitrogen and phosphate, but with little potash, which is often added as the chemical potassium chloride, so beware!
Analysis: N 6%, P 7%.

Hoof and horn   One of the best sources of slow-release nitrogen with a small amount of phosphate.
Analysis: N 14%, P 2%.
Available at most garden centres.

Fish meal and fish, blood and bone can both be made up into general fertilizers (fertilizers containing N, P and K in roughly similar concentrations) by adding powdered rock potash which contains 10% potash, which is quick releasing if finely ground. Apply all these fertilizers sparingly. A tablespoon of dried blood around a lettuce plant will pick it up after a cold spring. Fish, blood and bone can go on the soil as a general dressing at 100g (4oz) per metre/yard (about two handfuls). Hoof and horn is slower acting, but can go on in the same quantities. Bonemeal is very slow acting, and is usually used as phosphate for perennial plants.

Seaweed—plant food from the sea

Seaweed is the organic gardener's dream fertilizer, capable of helping him boost the life and health of soil and plants at almost every turn. The soil of the Aran Islands, off the west coast of Eire, is made of nothing but composted seaweed and sand.

Seaweed fertilizer is almost alive itself. Besides major plant nutrients (N, P and K), alginates and an abundance of trace elements, some forms also contain enzymes which are catalysts to the biological activity of the soil. Alginates can help build soil structure similar to the way earthworms help create soil crumbs. Many organic growers use seaweed simply because it works, without perhaps knowing exactly why they get the results they do. Calcified seaweed, in particular, registers poorly on standard analysis, but commercial growers would not waste their hard earned money on something if they did not believe in its value.

Seaweed comes in different forms, depending on which seaweed has been collected, and the way it has been prepared. They are:

Fresh seaweed is a complete fertilizer in itself, particularly rich in potash, the great love of potatoes, tomatoes and most other heavy fruiting plants. Some gardeners lay seaweed directly into the trench dug for their potatoes, or use as a mulch around tomato plants. It can also be added to the compost heap, or composted on its own in great heaps, like those on Aran. However, it can take up to two years for these heaps to break down. The salt content from the seaweed is not usually high enough to cause any problems.

Seaweed meal is bladder seaweed harvested without killing the roots so that the stock will regrow. It is then dried, ground and bagged. It's as close to a complete fertilizer as organic gardeners have, with much more than any chemical fertilizer could ever hope to contain, such as: trace elements, enzymes and other proteins, amino acids, carbohydrates, fats and vitamins. Use as a general fertilizer (about 100g (4oz) per square metre/yard), as an activator in the compost heap, or add to your potting mixture. Spread on the soil, it should be lightly dug in to prevent it forming a jelly-like surface layer.

Analysis: approximately N 2%, P 0.3%, K 2.3%.

Calcified seaweed is made from crushed granules of the coldwater coral Lithothamnium Calcareum. It is not as expensive as seaweed meal, but lacks the nitrogen and has less potash. Used mainly as a general soil improver and for correcting the pH of soils that have a tendency towards acidity. (Calcified seaweed is much better than lime for correcting pH because it will only correct soil acidity up to pH 6, so there is little chance of overliming.) Apply yearly about 100g (4oz) per square metre/yard.

Analysis: CaO (calcium oxide) 45–50%, MgO (magnesium oxide) 5–8%, P 0.35%, K 0.2%.

Liquid seaweed extract is made from one or more seaweed varieties. Some brands are more expensive than others because they use a more complicated extraction process which does not damage or destroy valuable enzymes. It is perhaps the most convenient plant food for the small space organic gardener as its riches can simply be poured straight out of a bottle. All are rich in major plant nutrients and trace elements including boron, bromine, chromium, cobalt, copper, iodine, manganese, molybdenum, nickel, silver, sodium, tungsten, titanium and vanadium. Many also contain hormones and vitamins. They are the best tonic for a plant suffering from an unknown disease, or just as a foliar feed to boost growth. Dilute according to the directions and spray on leaves once or twice a week during summer when growth is most rapid. Do not spray before rain or the feed will wash off before the plant has taken it in. Potatoes and tomatoes benefit particularly in terms of yields and flavour.

Analysis: approximately N 0.5%, P 0.25%, K 2%.

SEVENTEEN

Spacesavers

In a small garden it is important to get the most out of every inch of ground. This is now possible using simple techniques that work to maximize Gaia's potential in your garden—techniques that are part of developing organic systems, with their aim of producing sustainable yields greater than any chemical approach, and certainly of higher quality. The techniques described in this chapter work by making the most of available soil space; creating the conditions where the fastest growth is possible; keeping your garden full year-round; and ensuring continuity so that space is not wasted with a glut of more vegetables than you can eat at one time.

SPACESAVERS

Aim:
to maximize small garden space for maximum high quality yields.

What we can do:
★ make most use of soil space ★ maximize rate of growth ★ fill garden all year round ★ avoid gluts through continuity

How we can do it:
★ transplanting ★ successional cropping ★ companion planting ★ cloches

---

Let's see how it is done.

Spacesaver one: transplanting

Many crops, like courgettes (zucchini) and leeks, can be started off in a seedtray or small pot and transplanted out into the garden later in their development. Transplanting can dramatically increase the crops we can harvest from any given area of land, often with no more effort than before. This is possible for two reasons:

1 We can grow more crops each season as each plant spends less time in the ground. You do not have to wait for one harvest to sow the next. For instance, by the time you have cleared the ground of early potatoes, pot-raised spring onions (scallions) are already 7.5cm (3in) high and ready to go into the ground.

2 Frost sensitive plants can be started off indoors long before conditions are right for them outside.

Transplanting brings the seedtray germination and potting on techniques of The Indoor Garden into use outside. Details of the vegetables which thrive on transplanting are given under the individual vegetable headings. For most varieties, like courgettes (zucchini) and outdoor tomatoes, we will only need a few plants, which we can easily raise in 8.5cm (3½in) plastic pots, but with other varieties like lettuce or spring onions (scallions), we may want to grow in greater numbers. An inexpensive way of doing this is to make your own paper pots. These pots are not reusable, but for some plants (like spring onions (scallions) or parsley), whose roots have difficulty binding the soil in a pot, they are a positive advantage over plastic pots as the whole pot is planted out, where the plant roots easily push through the paper walls as they disintegrate into the soil. They can be simply made with just a newspaper, 8.5cm (3½in) diameter bottle, glue (or a stapler), scissors, and a seedtray.

Open out a sheet of newspaper if it is tabloid size, or fold large sheets in half. Lie your bottle along the longest edge, and roll the newspaper around it. Glue the opposite edge to secure. Now slide the bottle out of the roll and cut into 10cm (4in) sections. Staple each bottomless pot if it needs extra binding, and put one in a seedtray. Fill with 2.5cm (1in) of compost to keep its shape, and then do the same with the other pots until the tray is full. Finish filling the pots with compost and firm down to 1cm (½in) from their rim. Put the whole seedtray in 2.5cm (1in) of water for a few minutes to moisten the compost—and sow your seed!

The roots of each plant will start to grow through the newspaper before you plant out, so be careful not to destroy your pots as you remove them to their new home.

Make your own paper pots

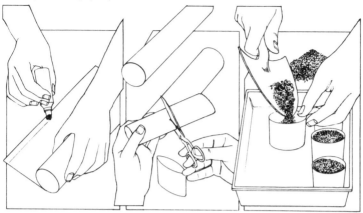

Roll a newspaper around a bottle. Secure with glue

Slide bottle out of roll and cut pots to required length

Place pots in seed tray and fill. Pinch out seedlings one to each pot

Spacesaver two: successional crops

Crop after crop ... that is the aim of Gaiaculture, and there is no reason why we cannot harvest two or three crops a year as long as we keep the soil well fed and ensure a constant variety of vegetables. The secret is to plan a succession of crops to avoid both idle land and great gluts of vegetables that will never be used. One grower managed to get this down to a fine art, (and made himself a fortune), by dividing his land into one yard squares and making sure each square was replanted within twenty four hours of the last harvest. For most of us, successional cropping can never be an exact science, mainly because of fluctuations in the weather, but there are a few tips that can help us get the most out of our love affair with Gaia.

Temperature is one of the most important factors governing plant development. As a general rule of thumb, plant growth doubles with every 10°C (18°F) rise in temperature, which accounts for the spurt of growth in spring. This means, for example, that if we want a regular supply of lettuce throughout the season, we will have to sow more and more frequently up to midsummer, as we find crops maturing faster with the increase in temperature. In contrast, if we made no allowance for temperature increase and sowed lettuce once a fortnight, the first spring crops would perhaps mature in succession, but by midsummer we would be faced with a glut as later sowing caught up with earlier ones, maturing all at the same time. And after the glut, we would be left with no lettuce at all.

Good husbandry Plants will grow fast to maturity if we give them what they want. A fine, moist seedbed, full of organic matter to prevent 'capping', ensures fast and even germination. Kept free of weeds (which rob them of nutrients and sunlight), protected from pests (which slow growth) and from the fury of the wind, plants will bring their harvests in on time. And that means we can better plan when one crop will finish and the next can go in.

Crop knowledge unfolds the wonders of each individual vegetable variety whose qualities can play an important role in filling our garden. For instance, 'evercropping' vegetables like swiss chard will give your twelve months of service from one sowing. So will parsley. Many cut-and-come-again crops like chicory, redico, endive and lettuce, are far less prone to gluts and shortages than other crops harvested at one go. Butterhead lettuce will not hold its heart for more than a few days in hot weather before it bolts, whereas a single sowing of a cut-and-come-again variety can keep you in lettuce leaves for months. Many of these 'evercropping' plants are also winter hardy, which means they can fill your garden when other vegetables just would not survive.

Crop knowledge can also help us avoid gluts and shortages, and provide a continuity of harvests throughout the season. A good example of this is the fact that the development of peas, cauliflowers, broad beans (fava beans), onions, French beans, and brussels sprouts is controlled by the amount of daylight. This has enabled plant breeders to create varieties that will always mature in the same order, a factor we can use to ensure continuity. For instance, if four varieties of peas—*Hurst Beagle, Hurst Canice, Victory Freezer* and *Hurst Greenshaft*—are all sown on the same day, they will all mature in succession over a period of a few weeks. In contrast, other crops, like spring onions (scallions), will give us continuity from regular sowings of just one variety.

Spacesaver three: companion planting

Companion planting helps to keep plants healthy and free from disease. We will take a better look at these benefits in the next chapter.

Companion planting can also help us get the most out of our garden by placing different vegetables side by side so that they make the best use of sunlight, nutrients and, most of all, space.

There are two main ways companion planting works: a fast growing plant between a slow growing one before it needs all the space, or different shaped plants that do not compete for sunlight.

Salad crops usually make the best fast growers to intercrop between slower plants. For instance, radish between carrot or beetroot (beet) rows, or lettuce between broad beans (fava beans) or cabbage, and you can easily get a crop of spring onions (scallions) between leeks before they start to grow away.

On the other hand sunflowers deep in the courgette (zucchini) or pumpkin patch are so tall they make no difference to yields below. Endive thrive under the tall stalks of brussels sprout plants, and it is an old garden practice to put broad beans (fava beans) in the same row as potatoes—but make sure you can harvest the beans before the potatoes are ready! Plant out your late leeks among your early peas. Cut the peas down when they are finished instead of digging them up and their nitrogen will feed the leeks.

Intercropping can help make maximum use of your space, but it cannot work miracles. If plants are too close together they will be like weeds to each other and give smaller yields. You need to experiment in order to discover what is and is not possible.

Spacesaver four: spacing methods

Sowing plants in rows wide apart is a legacy from field scale crops kept clean with horse drawn hoes—hardly the recipe for the small space garden! Experiments at National Vegetable Research Station, and HDRA, have found that *staggered spacing*, with plants put out *equidistant* to each other, is the best spacing pattern. That means that every plant is the same distance from its neighbours in all directions and no space is lost by the gap between rows. Each plant will form a triangle with those next to it.

Details of staggered spacing only give one distance for planting out, instead of distance between plants, and distance between rows. You can either stagger plants by thinning rows so that plants are equidistant to each other (remember to sow the rows closer together in the first place), or by planting out to those spacings.

Some plants still do best in rows, especially root crops like carrots

Equidistant spacing saves space between rows

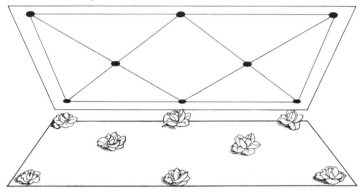

and parsnips which cannot be transplanted as seedlings, but these can be planted much closer together if you stay on top of the weeds. For instance, I grew carrots on a field scale with 65cm (26in) between drills for easy tractor hoeing, whereas most gardening books recommend rows 30cm (12in) apart. But in Holland I saw intensive market gardens crop beautiful early carrots in rows just 15 cm (6in) apart, 18cm (7in) for maincrop varieties. Now that is really getting intense!

Other research has shown that maximum yields come from much closer spacings than would produce the largest vegetables. Small is beautiful—it is the source of abundance! You will find details under each individual crop heading.

Spacesaver five: cloches

Cloches save space because they boost plant growth and because they allow us to grow on soil that would normally be too cold for crops in autumn and spring. If plant growth generally doubles for every 10°C (18°F) rise in temperature, no wonder protected lettuce can heart three weeks earlier and early potatoes can come out two weeks sooner. But cloches are more than a mini-greenhouse that collects heat. They also protect from frost and the ravages of the wind. They keep birds, cats and dogs off our crops, and some even act as a welcome barrier against slugs.

In warmer climates it may not be worth investing in cloches as they tend to be expensive, but in temperate climates that plunge into winter each year, they can boost production dramatically. There are many different kinds to choose from:

Glass cloches are the traditional 'tent' or 'barn' cloche made from two sheets of glass joined with special clips. Available from many garden centres.

Corrugated PVC sheeting, bent in a semi-circle and held in place with wire loops, lets in plenty of light. Make sure they are firmly secured or they may take off in high winds and shatter. Available from garden centres.

Polypropylene cloches are opaque, but still allow enough light for plant growth. Made out of rigid polypropylene they are very sturdy and stack together for easy storage. I like them because they usually come with endplates as well which gives those first spring lettuce excellent protection against slugs.

Floating film is a sheet of polythene film which is often perforated. It is laid over your crops with the edges secured into the soil. As the plants grow, they create their own space by pushing the light film up. A very good, cheap source of early crop protection. Ultra-violet light finally weakens the film so that it tears, but with care you can use the same sheet for two or three seasons. Perforated film lets the plants breathe and allows some rainwater to get through without loss of heat. Best used for fast growing plants like potatoes, broad beans (fava beans), and lettuce. I find it a nuisance with slow growing crops like carrots because the film has to be removed every few days to weed.

EIGHTEEN

Vegetable Varieties

Broad beans (fava beans)   A good, easy-to-grow crop for newly cleared ground. Roots supply nitrogen to the soil. Broad beans shelter other crops from the wind, or make a good screen in front of a fence or unsightly part of the garden. Sow 4–5cm (1½–2in) deep between late winter and mid-spring for harvesting from early to late summer, or raise indoors in early spring in paper pots and transplant when seedlings are 10cm (4in) high. Choose *The Sutton*, or *The Midget* dwarf varieties for small spaces, or a *Longpod* variety for taller growth. Harvest while still young (very young pods can be cooked whole like french beans, and tender beans are deliciously sweet eaten raw in salads). Grow at 25cm (10in) equidistant spacing, or 2.5cm (1in) apart in 30cm (12in) rows. Or even sow them in the same drill as maincrop potatoes. All beans also do well grown with carrots or cauliflower. If blackfly becomes a problem, pinch out the growing tip or spray with soapy water.

French beans   Another easy-to-grow delicacy, but frost sensitive and will not germinate in cold soil, so either sow indoors in early spring, under cloches in late spring, or in the open from late spring until early summer. Plant out at 23cm (9in) equidistant spacing, or 5cm (2in) apart in 45cm (18in) rows, 4–5cm (1½–2in) deep. *The Prince*, or *Tendergreen* are good varieties for all sowings. Plants will grow 40–50cm (16–20in) high. Pick beans as soon as they are ready as this induces the plant to produce more. Keep free of weeds and prevent from drying out with either a mulch or plenty of water in the evening.

Runner beans are easiest grown with outdoor sowings 4–5cm (1½–2in) deep in early summer using a variety like *Achievement, Enorma* or *Hammonds Dwarf Scarlet* which only grows about 40cm (16in) high. Start harvesting from midsummer. The harvest date can be brought forward two weeks by indoor sowing in paper pots in late spring, or under cloches in early summer. Plant out or remove protection only after the last frost in a double row 60cm

(2 feet) apart with 15cm (6in) between plants. Apart from the dwarf varieties, runner beans need support from canes, netting, the garden fence or wall trellis. They all need sunlight and shelter from the wind.

Beetroot (beet) can be available year-round from a combination of early and maincrop varieties. Sow earliest crops 1–2cm (½–¾in) deep in clusters of 2–3 seeds per paper pot indoors at the end of winter, or outside from early spring, again either in clusters at 30cm (12in) equidistant spacing, or in rows 18cm (7in) apart and 10cm (4in) between plants for *Avonearly* or *Bolthardy* varieties. Harvest in late spring as soon as the globes are large enough and use the tops in salads or sautéed like spinach. For autumn and overwintered crops, make one sowing of *Cheltenham Greentop* in late spring at 12.5cm (5in) equidistant spacing or in rows 30cm (12in) apart, 5cm (2in) between plants. Protect against slugs, and boost growth with a liquid seaweed spray. In late autumn store the crop in the ground under a thick mulch of straw, or harvest by twisting off the tops and storing, unwashed, in paper sacks in a cool dark place. In this way beetroot will keep until spring. Beetroot grows well next to lettuce or members of the onion family.

Brassica (includes cabbage, cauliflower, curly kale, winter and summer broccoli, and brussels sprouts). All are hungry plants requiring high levels of organic matter, and good firm ground so that their root systems are not dislodged by the wind. Broadcast seed in a fine seedbed, one tenth of the garden area they will finally take up, (under a cloche for early crops), and transplant when seedlings are 7.5–15cm (3–6in) tall. Plant by twisting off the topmost leaves of the seedlings (not the growing tip), and dropping into a dibbled hole 5–7.5cm (2–3in) deep. Water and press the root firmly down with your foot. Initially the plants will look wilted and very sorry for themselves, but recover in a couple of days. Spacing will determine the size of the plant—for larger plants use larger spacing than given below. Always rotate brassica (including swedes and turnips), so they are never grown on the same plot more than one year in four to avoid clubroot. Leaf-eating caterpillars, and flea beetle on outdoor sown cotyledons, are dealt with in the Banishing Pests chapter.

Spring cabbage varieties such as *Durham Elf* or *Pixie* can be sown in midsummer for transplanting in late summer. They should be spaced 20–30cm (8–12in) apart and can be harvested from early spring.

Summer cabbages (eg *Hispie*) should be sown early-mid-spring. Transplant them 20–30cm (8–12in) apart at the end of spring for harvesting from early to late summer. In the middle of spring sow winter cabbages such as *Ice Queen Savoy* or *Dutch Winter White*. Transplant them in midsummer 38–45cm (15–18in) equidistantly and harvest them from early winter onwards.

Mini cauliflowers can be sown in early-late spring and are ready for eating from early summer through to late autumn. They need to be transplanted when the plants are 12.5cm (4in) high and should be spaced 15cm (6in) apart. Kale should be sown in the middle of spring and should be transplanted when the seedlings are 12.5cm (4in) high, spacing them 38cm (15in) apart. They are ready for harvesting from the end of summer right through to early spring. Winter broccoli, such as *Early Purple Sprouting*, needs to be sown in mid-spring for harvesting about 12 months later. Transplant when 12.5cm (4in) high and space 45cm (18in) apart. Summer broccoli (calabrese), such as *Green Comet*, should be sown in early-mid-spring 25cm (10in) apart. It does not need transplanting and can be harvested from early summer until the first frosts arrive. Brussels sprouts should be sown in early spring and transplanted when 12.5cm (4in) high, spacing them 60–90cm (24–36in) apart. The *Peer Gynt* variety is ready for harvesting from later autumn, while *Rampart* will last right through the winter until early spring.

Carrots dislike fresh organic manure which forks their roots. Early varieties like *Amsterdam Forcing* and *Early Nantes* can be sown in early spring for new season carrots in early summer. *Chantenay Red-Core* is a flavourful variety for sowing in spring, while *Autumn King* or *Berlicum* are sown from mid-spring until the early summer for winter storage. All varieties need a fine, well dug seedbed. Sow direct into the ground, 1cm (½in) deep, summer varieties 15 seeds per 30cm (12in), in rows 18cm (7in) apart, and winter varieties 15 seeds per 30cm (12in), in rows 25cm (10in) apart. Do not thin seedlings, even if you have sown too thickly, as this attracts carrot root fly. Begin to weed as soon as the thin cotyledons become visible, about 14 days after sowing.

Attracted by scent, the rootfly lays its eggs in the maturing root early summer, and to a lesser extent, in late summer. When the eggs hatch, tiny maggots feed on the roots, discolouring them, and turning the leaves a reddish hue, Summer carrots, harvested by midsummer, will not be troubled by rootfly because the eggs will not yet have hatched, but for later crops avoid the pest either by surrounding your crop with a polythene barrier 60cm (2 feet) high (rootfly fly close to the ground), or delay sowing until the early summer when the main threat has passed and avoid disturbing the seedlings in any way as this may spread the carrot scent. Garlic and onions planted close by also help by masking the scent. Store winter carrots like beetroot (beet) and they will keep until spring.

Chicory For the new chicory varieties see the Indoor Garden. *Witloof* chicory is the standard 'forcing variety' whose blanched chicons make a welcomed salad vegetable in winter. Sow seed 1cm (½in) deep in rows 20cm (8in) apart with 12 seeds per row anytime in spring. The seeds will germinate easily and grow through the summer with little attention apart from the occasional hoeing. In early winter lift the roots with a fork so as not to damage them. Throw away any forked roots, and any with less than 1cm (½in) or more than 2.5cm (1in) width across the crown. Cut away all leaves cleanly 1cm (½in) from the crown and trim the root to 12.5cm (5in) in length. Store in paper sacks in a cool, dark, frostfree environment. At regular intervals throughout the winter, remove a few roots and bury them close together in peat 13cm (6in) deep and place in gentle heat. Within 4–6 weeks, according to the temperature, they will have sprouted the white chicons we see in the shops. Harvest with a sharp knife and throw the spent roots on the compost heap.

Sugarloaf is a 'self blanching' chicory which looks something like a cross between the chicons of *Witloof* chicory and *Chinese Cabbage*. Reasonably hardy, they are a useful salad vegetable in early winter. Sow seeds in rows 18cm (7in) apart, 10cm (4in) between plants 1cm (½in) deep in early summer. Firm hearts will be ready by late autumn. Protect from frost with a good mulch of straw until they are needed, through to early winter. A broadcast crop for harvest on a cut-and-come-again basis can make salad leaves available all year round from one sowing in spring. Protect with cloches during winter.

Courgettes (zucchini) and marrows are best started indoors, and planted out after the last frost. (See *The Indoor Garden* for details.) If there is still some risk of frost, protect with either cloches or a floating polythene film until the first flowers appear. The plants benefit from a well manured, well watered, mulched bed, able to maintain the correct conditions for growth throughout the summer. As soon as the courgette fruit are 10–15cm (4–6in) long, break them off the plant stem at their base—harvesting will induce further fruit formation and keep the plant producing until the first autumn frosts. Slugs can damage the fruit, but this can be reduced if the fruit is supported off the ground with either straw or an upturned pot.

Garlic can be grown from store-bought cloves, broken up into their segments and pressed into the soil 10cm (4in) apart between autumn and early spring. Prepare the ground to a fine tilth, with a good dressing of compost, and plant early to ensure large cloves. Like onions, garlic will not tolerate weeds. Harvest in midsummer when top growth has died off by pulling up the cloves and leaving them to dry in a warm place.

Land cress is an underrated small garden salad crop that is fast growing, available all year round, and happy in shaded or north facing aspects of the garden. Sow the first seed between early spring and early summer 1cm (½in) deep, 15 seeds per 30cm (12in) in rows 23cm (9in) apart. Harvest individual leaves as needed throughout the summer, and sow again in midsummer for winter supplies. Protect in winter with straw or clothes for better growth.

Leeks provide excellent continuity in the garden because they are available over a long season (when other crops are in short supply), and will stand mature for months without going to seed. What is more, they can be grown the size to suit your needs merely by altering the plant spacing—for large leeks use 23cm (9in) equidistant spacing, but for smaller, higher yielding plants, reduce the equidistant spacing down to 7.5cm (3in). Sow leeks in a seedbed like brassica in early to mid-spring, or if you only require a few plants, sow half a dozen seeds in a 7.5cm (3in) pot. Whichever way, cover the seeds with a damp cloth, or piece of black plastic until they germinate in order to conserve moisture. Plant out in early summer into richly manured ground. Trim the top leaves and roots of each plant before placing in a 7.5cm (3in) dibbled hole at the desired spacing, and watering in. Use a variety like *Autumn Mammoth*, or *Early Market* for an autumn harvest, and *Musselburgh* for anytime between midwinter and spring. Leeks grow well next to carrots, onions and celery.

Lettuce can either be grown as hearted plants, or in a bed and harvested on a cut-and-come-again basis (see *The Indoor Garden* for details). Continuity is easier to achieve using the second method. Continuity for hearted plants relies on successional sowings of varieties suited to each individual season, and the use of cloches or polythene film in spring and autumn. The simplest method is to start the season in the early spring with store-bought butterhead seedlings planted at an equidistant spacing of 23cm (9in) apart. These will be ready by late spring. Continue planting a few plants every few days (but more frequently as temperatures increase—see the previous chapter). Cos and crisphead varieties can be planted out from late spring. They are slower maturing than butterhead, but do not bolt as easily. The last unprotected seedlings can be planted out in midsummer from a variety like *Valdor* or *Winter Density*. Slugs, aphids, and botrytis can affect plants—see *Banishing Pests* (chapter 19) for methods of control. Plants in spring cold spells benefit from a teaspoon of dried blood to help boost their growth.

Onions give reliable crops grown from 'sets' (small, immature onions grown the year before), available from garden centres and hardware stores. Choose a variety like *Stuttgarter Giant* or *Sturon*. Plant out into a well fertilized bed in early spring, in rows 18cm (7in) apart, 5cm (2in) between bulbs. This close spacing helps weeding because it means we do not have to weed in between individual bulbs, but only along the row. Onions start to mature after the longest day whatever their size as the control mechanisms are governed by daylight length. By midsummer leaf growth should have died back. Lift the onions and leave to dry out on the ground if it is dry, or remove them to somewhere warm. In early autumn store the crop in trays, net bags or onion strings.

Springs onions (scallions) have a long growing season if we start them off indoors sown in clumps of up to 15 seeds per 7.5cm (3in) pot. When the seedlings are 10cm (3–4in) high, transplant the entire pot at 12.5cm (5in) equidistant spacing. The first pots can be sown in late winter and can continue until midsummer. Alternatively, sow rows of spring onions 2.5cm (1in) wide, 1cm (1in) deep, amongst other crops like cabbage or carrots anytime after early spring. Weed with vigour and harvest as required.

Parsley See *The Indoor Herb Garden* (chapter 11) for germination details, or sow in early spring 1cm (½in) deep, in a row and thin plants to 10cm (4in) apart. Closer spacing only produces more stalk and less leaf. Harvest a few leaves at a time from each plant, always leaving enough for continued growth. Keep parsley away from carrots as its scent attracts the carrot rootfly which does not damage the parsley, but can cause havoc among the carrots. Parsley is a biennial plant and will survive most winters if its leaves are cut back in autumn before the first heavy frosts.

Potatoes are divided into early and maincrop varieties. Both are extremely useful in helping to clear new land because their cultivation and harvest requires the soil to be turned several times, and their rapid growth competes with even the strongest weeds. Maincrop varieties include *Desiree, King Edward*, and *Maris Piper*. Sow the tubers in well manured ground 12.5cm (5in) deep at 30cm (12in) equidistant spacing in mid-spring. Black polythene laid over the bed after planting aids rapid growth by warming the soil. After 4 weeks you will notice bulges under the polythene where the young shoots have broken through the soil. Instead of removing the polythene, simply cut a hole at each bulge and allow the potato shoot to come through—the polythene will now help weed control and prevent new tubers turning green from exposure to sunlight. Regular foliar feeds of liquid seaweed will boost growth and help thicken the leaf cuticles against blight. Harvest potatoes in September when the leaves have died down. Use any damaged tubers immediately, and store the rest in paper sacks, keeping them cool, dry and free from frost. Potato blight, slugs and wireworm are common pests—see *Banishing Pests* (chapter 19) for methods of control.

Early varieties include *Ulster Sceptre, Maris Bard, Wilja*, and *Arran Pilot*. Between early autumn and midwinter, place the tubers in dutch tomato trays or similar boxes in a dry, frost free environment. The aim is to induce the plants to start their growth before they are planted out.

Ideally, by the early spring each tuber should have a thick green shoot 1–2cm (½–¾in) long. The rate of growth can be controlled largely by temperature. The shoots will also grow most rapidly in dark conditions, but will lack the strength of a green shoot grown in daylight. Plant the tubers with care, shoot uppermost, 23cm (9in) equidistant spacing. Black plastic, or a polythene floating film, will advance your harvest date by up to two weeks. In sheltered areas the first early potatoes can be dug in early summer. Clear the ground quickly, (while potato prices are still high in the shops), for another crop like late leeks, spring cabbage, or summer lettuce.

Radish see *The Indoor Garden*.

Shallots are grown from bulbs similar to onion sets, except that each bulb will sprout up to eight green shoots. the shoots can be harvested early and used as spring onions (scallions) in late spring from 5cm (2in) equidistant spacing, (see *The Indoor Garden* for details), or left to mature into the same number of bulbs in midsummer in rows 20cm (8in) apart, 15cm (6in) between bulbs. Treat the same as onion sets.

Spinach can often be cropped year round in mild years, but takes more labour than the hardier Swiss Chard and Perpetual Spinach (for cultivation details see below) that are gradually replacing this crop in low-maintenance, small space gardens. Having said that, summer spinach grows well as a catch crop in the shade of taller plants like beans or brassica. Sow at 2–3 week intervals between spring and midsummer 2cm (¾in) deep in 30cm (12in) rows and thin plants to 7.5cm (3in) apart. Spinach needs a moisture retentive soil, rich in organic matter. Mulch young plants, or water frequently during the summer. Harvest the larger outer leaves of each plant from late spring to autumn. Winter spinach needs a well drained, open site to sow the seeds in late summer in rows 30cm (12in) apart with 23cm (9in) between plants. For best results protect winter spinach with cloches from mid-autumn onwards. Varieties for both summer and winter sowings include *Jovita* and *Sigmaleaf*.

Sweetcorn needs a long growing season and good pollination for full ears of corn. Start the plants indoors during early spring with two seeds per 7.5cm (3in) paper pot. Pinch out weakest seedling, and leave the other to grow on until hardening off and transplanting in early summer when the last risk of frost has passed. In order to ensure good pollination, plant sweetcorn in blocks rather than long rows, at an equidistant spacing of 38cm (15in), and a minimum of a dozen plants. Water well and keep weeds down. In a good summer the earliest harvests will be ready by midsummer. Pick cobs while they are still 'milky', before they become over-mature. Try *Kelvedon Sweetheart* and *Northern Belle* varieties.

Swiss chard (Seakale beet) provides year round continuity from two sowings. It grows in practically any soil, but prefers plenty of organic matter. Sow two seeds 1cm (½in) deep at 23cm (9in) equidistant spacings in early spring, and prick out all but the strongest seedling at each station. Start picking the outside leaves in midsummer and sow again for continuity into next spring. Spring growth will be quickened by a top dressing of complete fertilizer applied 50g (2oz) per square metre/yard. Perpetual spinach has larger, fleshier leaves than ordinary spinach and should be treated like Swiss Chard.

Tomatoes see *The Indoor Garden*.

NINETEEN

Banishing Pests

The organic gardener has two defences against pests. The first is the health of the soil which deals with 90% of the problems. The remaining 10% are dealt with by Integrated Pest Management (IPM)— various techniques working together to reduce or eliminate pest damage.

IPM works with the entire web of life that makes up your garden. Disease or pests are signs of imbalance within the whole life matrix— not an excuse to exterminate a species and harm countless others with chemical poisons. The different techniques of IPM are ways we can alter the web of life in our garden to restore balance to the whole, while causing minimum possible damage to other parts of the web. With IPM there is often more than one way to deal with any pest. The most elegant are the 'invisible' controls like rotation, companion planting, and caring for the local hedgehog—they are the subtle ways of adjusting the balance of nature. You will find details for specific crops under their individual headings in the previous chapter. Now let us look at the broad outlines of IPM:

Rotation Nature loves variety and hates monoculture. Many pesticides are used today as the result of the build-up of pest and disease through monoculture that gives no break in the life-cycle of many of these organisms. Rotation means 'rotating' crops around your garden so that no crop sees the same ground for three or four years. Brassica (plus swede (rutabaga) and turnip) are perhaps the most important garden crop to rotate to avoid *clubroot*—a disease carried in the soil which deforms their roots and stunts growth. (Once a soil has clubroot it is practically impossible to get rid of, even with chemicals.)

Rotations also help maintain soil fertility. Some plants like potatoes are heavy feeders, while others like carrots fork in well manured ground. Both can have what they want if we manure at one stage in the rotation.

A typical four year rotation is:

Year one: POTATOES
Year two: LEGUMES   (peas and beans)
Year three: BRASSICAS   (cabbage family, with swede
                            (rutabaga) and turnips)
Year four: ROOTS   (onions, carrots, beetroot,
                            parsnips, courgettes (zucchini) ...)
(Lettuce crops are placed wherever they make the best use of space.)

If you have a small garden or you do not grow many brassica, your rotation can be less strict, especially if you have many different vegetable varieties all packed together.

Companion planting has been made famous by Louise Riotte's book *Carrots Love Tomatoes*. The more romance you can bring to your garden, the fewer pests there will be. Based more on experience than experiment, many love affairs go back years. Marigolds keep whitefly away from tomatoes and increase yields. Onions and garlic help keep carrot rootfly from carrots, and increase the flavour of lettuce. Nasturtium keep whitefly from cucumbers. More details under each crop heading in the previous chapter.

Sowing time   Many pests go through various stages of their life cycle at different times of the year. If we know this, we can sow our crops to miss the worst infestation, for example planting early potatoes to miss blight in wet years.

Different varieties often have different levels of resistance. *Desiree* is a maincrop potato variety with some resistance to blight, whereas good old *King Edward* has very little. Many lettuce plants are bred nowadays for resistance to mildews instead of yield.

Garden hygiene   Many common garden pests need protection in order to survive the winter. They find this in old bricks, stones, weeds and rotting vegetable matter. If your garden is clean and tidy, frost will kill many of your unwanted companions. Mildew fungi also overwinter in plant debris, while some lettuce viruses survive in weed seeds, so clear everything away, put it on the compost heap and deny them an early start next season. In summer keep the jungle well back from the vegetable patch—then if pests want your crops they will have to travel. An ordered garden gives no free housing to massed hordes before they descend.

Soil pH can help reduce some diseases. Potato scab is made worse by lime, whereas clubroot dislikes lime.

Biological controls Commercial growers have turned to Nature, who can succeed where the most deadly poisons have failed. Biological controls introduce a natural enemy to the pest to keep it under control at levels where it can do no serious damage. Interestingly, most controls will only work if the pest is also present, as its source of food or reproduction vehicle—without the pest there could be no pest control. Unfortunately (or fortunately) there probably are not enough pests in a small garden to make biological controls worthwhile, especially if you have to send away for the predators which are usually expensive and have to be used immediatley. However, you can always collect your own natural biological controls. For instance, a dozen ladybirds will help plants infested with aphids or blackfly. And if you can, tempt a friendly hedgehog into your garden with a saucer of milk put out in the evening—they are voracious consumers of slugs. Even the small violet ground beetle may get through a slug a day. There are many other beneficial creatures that share your small patch of Gaia who are more than willing to help pest control.

Organic sprays are non-synthetic sprays that breakdown rapidly into the biological cycles of the soil. The best are specific to a particular pest and perfectly safe for all other garden life, including us. Nicotine, however, kills bees and should be only used as a last resort. Let's look at the most useful safe insecticides, many of which we can make ourselves:

Safe organic sprays

Safe organic sprays play an important role in IPM, but they are only one method of pest control. Check to see if they are the best for you, or if you have just turned to them first out of habit.

Burgundy mixture is made from copper sulphate and washing soda. It kills the spores of potato blight on potatoes and tomatoes as a preventative measure. Bordeaux mixture is similar. Both are available from garden centres.

Derris comes from the root of the derris tree. It is harmless to bees, but kills the eggs and larvae of the two- and seven-spotted ladybird, so should be used with care. Good against caterpillars, aphids, some weevils, and flea-beetle. Available as a dust or liquid from garden

Soil pests

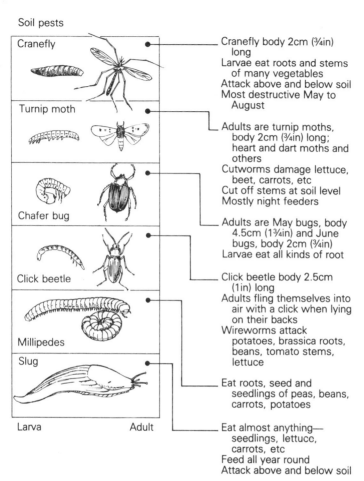

Cranefly

Turnip moth

Chafer bug

Click beetle

Millipedes

Slug

Larva   Adult

Cranefly body 2cm (¾in) long
Larvae eat roots and stems of many vegetables
Attack above and below soil
Most destructive May to August

Adults are turnip moths, body 2cm (¾in) long; heart and dart moths and others
Cutworms damage lettuce, beet, carrots, etc
Cut off stems at soil level
Mostly night feeders

Adults are May bugs, body 4.5cm (1¾in) and June bugs, body 2cm (¾in)
Larvae eat all kinds of root

Click beetle body 2.5cm (1in) long
Adults fling themselves into air with a click when lying on their backs
Wireworms attack potatoes, brassica roots, beans, tomato stems, lettuce

Eat roots, seed and seedlings of peas, beans, carrots, potatoes

Eat almost anything—seedlings, lettuce, carrots, etc
Feed all year round
Attack above and below soil

centres, but check the label first because some brands have been 'strengthened' with synthetic additives.

Elder spray you can make yourself to control aphids and small caterpillars. Put 450g (1lb) of elderleaves (from the elder tree that produces the strong scented white blossom in early summer and elderberries in late summer for elderberry jam) in an old saucepan with 3.4 litres (6 pints) of water. Bring to the boil and simmer for half an hour. Sieve and use cold and undiluted. Lawrence Hills says it will keep for three months if you seal the lid while the mixture is still hot.

Fertosan slug destroyer a welcomed herbal preparation that kills

Some beneficial insects and other creatures

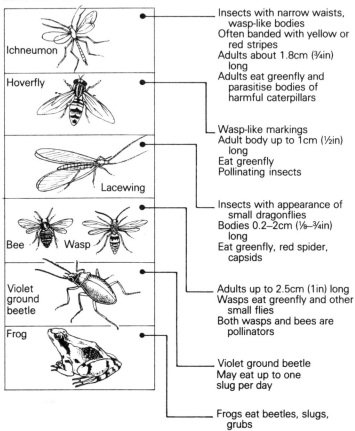

Ichneumon

Hoverfly

Lacewing

Bee Wasp

Violet ground beetle

Frog

Insects with narrow waists, wasp-like bodies
Often banded with yellow or red stripes
Adults about 1.8cm (¾in) long
Adults eat greenfly and parasitise bodies of harmful caterpillars

Wasp-like markings
Adult body up to 1cm (½in) long
Eat greenfly
Pollinating insects

Insects with appearance of small dragonflies
Bodies 0.2–2cm (⅛–¾in) long
Eat greenfly, red spider, capsids

Adults up to 2.5cm (1in) long
Wasps eat greenfly and other small flies
Both wasps and bees are pollinators

Violet ground beetle
May eat up to one slug per day

Frogs eat beetles, slugs, grubs

Toads are also beneficial

slugs on contact. Harmless to humans, birds, pets and earthworms. Available from garden centres.

Nettle spray—another homemade brew that helps repel a wide variety of pest by 'quickening' the life of the plants. Also good as a general tonic to boost plant vitality. Make the same way as Elder spray, or suspend a hessian sack of nettles in a barrel of water for two weeks and then spray.

Nicotine   One of stronger sprays, made from tobacco extract. Spares ladybird eggs, larvae, adults, and hoverfly larvae (who can eat 600 aphids before becoming adult). Kills bees, so spray in the evening when they are back in their hives. Nicotine is a good spray for red

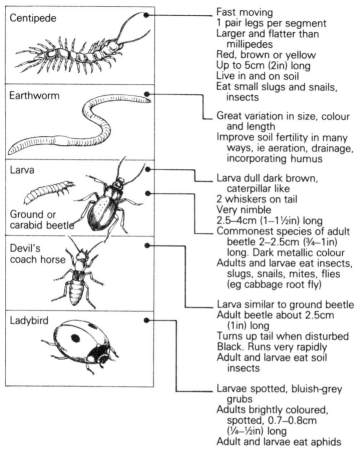

Centipede	Fast moving 1 pair legs per segment Larger and flatter than millipedes Red, brown or yellow Up to 5cm (2in) long Live in and on soil Eat small slugs and snails, insects
Earthworm	Great variation in size, colour and length Improve soil fertility in many ways, ie aeration, drainage, incorporating humus
Larva	Larva dull dark brown, caterpillar like 2 whiskers on tail Very nimble 2.5–4cm (1–1½in) long
Ground or carabid beetle	Commonest species of adult beetle 2–2.5cm (¾–1in) long. Dark metallic colour Adults and larvae eat insects, slugs, snails, mites, flies (eg cabbage root fly)
Devil's coach horse	Larva similar to ground beetle Adult beetle about 2.5cm (1in) long Turns up tail when disturbed Black. Runs very rapidly Adult and larvae eat soil insects
Ladybird	Larvae spotted, bluish-grey grubs Adults brightly coloured, spotted, 0.7–0.8cm (¼–½in) long Adult and larvae eat aphids

spider mite, caterpillars, and the tougher pests. Make your own by mixing cigarette ash with a bit of washing-up liquid in water, or buy as a 2% solution.

Pyrethrum is made from dried flower heads of certain chrysanthemums. Safe for warm blooded animals and most natural predators. Kills blackfly, aphids, caterpillars. Available from garden centres. Some have added synthetic pyrethroids which are not organic.

Quassia comes from the wood of certain trees from South America and the West Indies. Usually sold as quassia chips, they make a weak spray against aphids, small caterpillars and mites. Does not harm beneficial insects.

Soft soap is made from vegetable oils and potash. Good as a general cleanser and spray against aphids. Soap flakes, detergents, washing-up liquids and even washing-up water will kill aphids, but soft soap is the purest and most effective. Available from chemists.

The new nature regulators:

1 **Biodynamic preparations**   Special preparations for raising the vitality of plants, crop yield, long-term fertility, and the control of pests. Designed to be used as part of Rudolf Steiner's biodynamic method of organic growing. Available only to the members of the Biodynamic Agricultural Association.

2 **Homeopathic preparations** are still in their infancy as a science. The preparations from Solar Quest are made from selected seaweeds and herbs and homeopathically potentized. They can be used as a soil balancer, compost activator and for pest control.

Pest and disease control

Control for specific pests and diseases of individual vegetables are given in the previous chapter. Here we will just look at a dozen of the most common complaints in the garden. Remember, Gaia's health looks after 90% of any potential pest, we are only dealing with that remaining 10%.

Aphids are maybe the most common pest—and the easiest to get rid of with either one of the homemade sprays we have talked about, or simply old dishwater. Ladybirds will naturally congregate around aphids which are a succulent food supply for them. Each year organic cereal crops are black with aphids until the first battalions of ladybirds come over the hill.

Aphids suck the sap of plants. They are less of a problem in the organic garden, because cell walls naturally tend to be thicker. They can be strengthened even more with foliar feeds of liquid seaweed. Nasturtiums repel aphids both indoors and out in the garden.

Birds are a mixed blessing. China's harvests were devastated when the Central Committee decreed sparrows the enemy of the people because they were always in amongst the corn. In fact they were eating caterpillars and other pests, which rapidly took over when the sparrows were gone! Thankfully, sparrows can once again fly Chinese skies in safety.

Other birds can wreak havoc, especially pigeons on young cabbage plants. They, and other birds, also have a passion for pea and lettuce seedlings. I have never found bird scarers to be any good, except lines of thin cotton, magnetic tape, fishing line and the like, criss-crossed a couple of feet apart over the crop about 15cm (6in) above the ground. It seems birds do not see the strands which frighten them on contact.

Cloches and netting not only keep birds away, but caterpillar-producing butterflies, cats and dogs as well. The same netting can be used year after year. Peas and beans can get support and protection from hawthorn twigs planted over them.

Blight starved two million people in the 1845 Irish potato famine. It is a fungus whose air-borne spores destroy the foliage, stem and finally roots of potato and tomato plants. The only cure for both the chemical and organic gardener is prevention.

Blight only spreads in warm, moist conditions, so it will rarely attack a crop before early summer. This means early potato crops can usually be ready before the attack becomes severe. First signs of blight are round, dark brown blotches on the leaves, which spread and kill the entire leaf. By this time the spores have already germinated and penetrated the leaf—too late for control except to remove infected leaves (burn them) and stop the spread.

If conditions are right for blight then spray tomato and potato plants with Burgundy or Bordeaux mixture (see p. 134), which will kill any spores on the leaf before they germinate. You will have to repeat this every few days—especially after rain—for as long as blight conditions persist. Thickened cell walls will be more resistant to attack, so strengthen with foliar feeds. Some varieties of tomato and potato are *more* resistant to blight than others—an important consideration when you buy your seed. Indoors they are less likely to come in contact with the spores than those outside.

If your potato crops become infected beyond control, cut off the haulm (stem) just above soil before the fungus has a chance to travel down into the tubers and turn them into a useless mass of jelly. Cover the drills (rows) with earth or grass cuttings for more protection until you harvest. Pick green tomatoes, destroy the plant, and ripen the fruit indoors.

Botrytis is also called 'grey mould rot' and 'damping off'. Mainly a problem for young seedlings starting life in cold, damp conditions, (see *The Indoor Garden*). The secret is to keep the soil on the verge of drying out, and to have good ventilation. Can also affect spring and autumn lettuce. Give them some heat with a cloche, or a tablespoon of dried blood as a tonic and choose resistant varieties. Botrytis outside is usually a sign of poor health so check your soil!

Caterpillars can eat many plants down to a skeleton, but are mainly a problem on brassica, although brussels sprouts and winter broccoli seem unpopular with them. If you have only a few plants, check underneath their leaves every few days for clusters of white eggs which can be easily brushed off. Later on, pick the caterpillars off by hand and put them on the bird table where they will go down a treat.

You can prevent most infestations with netting over the plants. This stops butterflies laying their eggs in the first place.

Cats like to use containers and seedbeds as toilets. Protect with cloches and netting or moss, gravel and large pebbles in containers.

Fleabeetle is a common name for about half a dozen species of tiny beetles that eat young seedlings. They are most common on brassica, swede and turnip cotelydons (the leaves of a seedling that unfold from within the seed before the first true leaves emerge), but can also have a go at broad beans (fava beans) and peas. Do not confuse them with the much larger, beneficial ground beetles. Run your hand over a damaged crop and you will see dozens of small beetles jump out of the way, like fleas. They are the culprits and are most active in spring, and again in late summer (in the interval the females are laying eggs). The secret is to try to get plants past the cotyledon stage before these dates, or sow indoors in seedtrays and transplant. Derris, in powder or liquid form, kills them. Another method is to cover a board with some sticky substance like syrup or car oil and pass it over the row. As the beetles jump they will stick to the board.

Mildew shows up as tiny white dashes mainly on the leaves of onions and leeks. A little mildew on healthy organic plants will do no harm. If plants are unhealthy, there is a problem with your soil.

Red spider mite is a common indoor pest on all plants, including houseplants. The spiders are tiny red specks on the underside of the leaves. In large concentrations you will see silken webbing as well, but the first signs will be the plant looking ill with mottled and bronzed leaves. Encircle your plant with garlic cloves planted out to keep the mite away, (see the *Indestructible Vegetables* chapter), or introduce them to a few ladybirds. Derris and nicotine are also effective.

Slugs, like couch grass, always bring out the worst in me, while the truth is they play an important role recycling rotting organic matter, and spend only a small amount of their time among garden crops—even if it often seems that the world's slugs have converged on your lettuce!

Hygiene deprives them of their favourite habitats and food supply. Starlings, blackbirds, ground beetles, the Devil's coach-horse beetle and hedgehogs are the natural enemies of slugs, without whose help the situation would be much worse. Eggshells, soot and gravel will all hamper their efforts to get to your plants, and if you plant the next lettuce in a different part of your garden, the slugs will have to travel for food. Oakleaves are also said to help keep them away.

Slug destroyer can kill them on contact, or go out on a warm summer's evening, just as the light fades, and pick the slugs off your plants as they feed. Jack Temple, the organic gardening correspondent for *Here's Health* magazine, has found regular dressings of calcified seaweed brought his slug population under control.

Wireworm are the larvae of the click beetle. They are thin, orange and usually about 2cm (¾in) long with jaws at one end and a bulge at the other. They live in the soil for up to 5 years before they pupate. During this time they eat holes in root crops like potatoes, carrots and parsnips and in heavy infestations can kill other plants by destroying their root system. This is most frequent in gardens that have just come out of grass or pasture as wireworm do not like being disturbed by repeated cultivations, but if you have a lawn near your vegetable patch, they can migrate from there, even if your garden has been worked for years. For most gardens wireworm is not a problem, but if you have them, you'll soon know about it.

Early crops of carrots, beetroot and potatoes, if lifted before midsummer, should miss most of the wireworm as they do not start feeding seriously until the soil is properly warmed. If you find your garden infested, all you can do is lift your rootcrops early. If your garden has just come out of grass, the problem will be worse in the second year when there is less decomposing organic material for the creatures to eat, but numbers will fall off to acceptable levels by the fourth and fifth year.

Continuous cultivation and a green manure crop of mustard will quickly clear the ground. Mustard is their favourite food and they will eat so much that thousands will become beetles all at once and fly off to other pastures.

TWENTY

Weeds: Gaia's Guardians

Weeds!—the greatest single cause of poor yields, crop failure and frustration. And yet, we could not do without them. Gaia depends on them, while each year we spend huge sums of money spraying selective herbicides in an incessant war against them. The simple fact is that weeds are misunderstood. Seen in a different light, weeds add to the variety of our garden which is a sign of healthy land, aerate the soil with their roots, and bring up minerals from the subsoil. And right at the heart of the matter, weeds are Gaia's life pulse—a sign of her will to live. Ground that cannot support weeds is dead, and of no use in the continuing life cycle of the Earth. Without a canopy of green life, Gaia is exposed to the devastating effects of erosion and the leeching of valuable nutrients from the soil—a bare garden in winter can lose many of the nutrients we have so carefully composted.

So weeds are only doing a job—protecting the rich health of our soils. If we can protect our soils in some other way, weeds will leave us alone. Here are some suggestions:

Mulches work on the principle of covering the soil and inhibiting the germination of weeds. They are also the best organic means of clearing a garden of persistent perennial weeds like couch grass, nettles, docks and thistles which, like any other plant, cannot survive for long spells without light. One of the best gardens I have ever seen made extensive use of leaf mould, collected from beech trees in autumn, and used as a mulch throughout the summer around growing crops. But besides weed control, mulches have other properties that we can use in the garden. In general they act as insulators, preserving whatever soil conditions they were laid over. In winter this can help us protect crops from frost with a good layer of straw, but it also means that mulched soils are slower to warm up in spring which can delay plant growth. It is important, especially for water-loving crops like courgettes (zucchini), that we give the ground a good soaking before we lay the mulch, in order to avoid sowing our plants into a perpetual desert. Once mulched, a moist soil will resist drought in even the driest summers which cuts down watering time and helps prevent 'mid-day wilt'. Specific mulches have special qualities of their own, eg:

An old carpet is one of the best ways of eliminating perennial weeds. Cut back summer growth and lay in early Autumn while the soil is still warm. By late spring most perennials will have died through lack of light.

Black plastic can also be used to clear perennial weeds and as a bed mulch for transplanted or station planted vegetables like courgettes (zucchini) and runner beans. Just prepare your soil ready to receive the plants, and give the soil a good watering before laying the black plastic over the surface, with its edges tucked under the soil to stop it blowing away. Next, cut holes in the plastic at the appropriate intervals and plant out your crop. The same plastic can be used for a couple of years, although the ground will begin to turn 'sour' if left covered too long because the soil cannot breathe under the film. Black plastic is one of the few mulches that increase soil temperatures by absorbing the heat of the sun, which makes it useful for heat-loving crops like outdoor tomatoes. It is available from most garden centres.

Donaldson's Hortopaper is an ingenious mulch made from woodpulp and sphagnum peat that comes in an 8 metre roll, 80cm wide. When it is rolled out over a prepared bed, lettuce, tomato, sweetcorn or any other seedlings are simply pushed through the paper into the soil. At the end of the season the paper harmlessly decomposes into the soil. Somerset organic grower, Charles Dowding, uses hortopaper to great effect. Available at some garden centres and Donaldsons.

Newspaper can be your homemade hortopaper. Lay it several layers thick and water to keep it from blowing away. Newspaper is good for annual weeds, but not competition for hardy perennials like couch grass.

Straw can be laid around growing plants or on paths between beds, although it does tend to attract slugs. Do not use hay as it contains too many seeds.

Hedge-trimmings, grass cuttings or anything else biodegradable can be used as a mulch.

Green manures are a winter ground cover and suppress weeds.

Selective planting can reduce weeds. Fast growing plants like lettuce or potatoes cover your soil before most weeds have a chance, while companion planting can leave weeds with no space to grow. Other plants actually inhibit the growth of weeds. For instance, tomato plants are said to discourage couch grass.

A false seedbed is prepared two weeks in advance of the date you want to sow. Let the weeds germinate, then hoe and plant your seed.

Hoeing does not have to be a marathon task as long as weed seedlings are caught young, before they even look like causing trouble. Slow growing, row-sown crops, like carrots and beetroot (beet), will not survive the natural vigour of weeds without your help with the hoe. But do not waste your time unless conditions are dry so that weeds will wilt and die before they have a chance to re-root. Walk backwards as you hoe in order to avoid treading the seedlings back into the ground. Hoes come in many designs—I prefer the double edged, self sharpening Wolf hoes that are available from most garden centres.

Experimental research has shown that, if providing up to 10% of ground cover, weeds can actually *improve* yields. Nevertheless, keep your garden as weed-free as possible if you want to give your crops the conditions they deserve.

TWENTY-ONE

Time To Take Control

So there you have it. We have had a close look at the fast changing world we live in, the forces within it that continue to threaten our well-being, and the opportunities for positive change. And we have the information for one way we can begin to initiate that change ourselves, wherever we are, through the techniques of small space organic gardening. If you have liked what you have seen, then the only thing that remains is for you to take control and allow the *Quantum Carrot* approach to work for you. The control needs to be ours because we now realize that the *power* for positive change lies within us—a power we discover when we discard old habits that limit our potential, and begin to see ourselves at the centre of our world—our thoughts and actions creating the world we want. Right now there is a tested method that can help us get started.

It is called an Action Plan, and is based on our own answers to simple questions we can ask ourselves that will help make the *Quantum Carrot* Adventure a reality. The strength of an Action Plan comes from making sure all your answers are *measurable*, *achievable* and *time-related*. For instance, in answer to the question 'what kind of garden do I want?', my answer might be to start next week sprouting several varieties of sprouts, and by the end of the month to also have a window box planted up with herbs of my choice. This answer is a useful guide for me because, by the end of the week or month, I am able to measure my progress towards my goal. Given my present lifestyle, these goals are well within my reach; and I have definite times by which I hope to have my goals complete. At the end of the month I would review my Action Plan, see how I have got on, and make a new plan for next month. It is through simple steps like this that we get things done. You may like to write your Action Plan from your own questions, or base it on some of these:

★ What kind of garden do I want? What crops do I want to grow? When will I harvest my first crop?

★ What do I want my garden to do for me? How can I measure these changes?

★ What other step(s) do I want to take to create the life I want to live? How will I know when I have achieved it? How long do I think it will take?

Then, as part of putting your action plan into practice you may like to write down the answers to three other questions. They are:

★ What three qualities do I possess that give me the power to achieve what I want?

★ What is the greatest obstacle blocking my achievement of what I want?

★ What do I need to take the next step?

I hope you find these suggestions useful. Action plans are almost universal among people determined to get things done. Their beauty is that new ones can always take you on the next step of the way. Good luck!

References/Further Reading

Some of these titles are now out of print, but you should be able to obtain them through your library.

Chapter 1.   At the Leading Edge of Change

Lorenz, Konrad, *King Solomon's Ring*, Methuen, London, 1952

Mott, Lawrie, *Pesticides in Food—What the Public Needs to Know*, Natural Resources Defence Council Inc., San Francisco, 1984

Myers, Norman, *The Gaia Atlas of Planet Management*, Pan Books, London, 1985

Russell, Peter, *The Awakening Earth*, Ark Paperbacks, London, 1984

Salk, Jonas, *The Survival of the Wisest*, Harper & Row, New York, 1973

Chapter 2.   The Riches of the 80's

Goldsmith, Edward, 'Open letter to Mr Clausen, President of the World Bank', *The Ecologist*, Vol.15 No.1/2, 1985

Harris, George T., 'From Hedonism to Health', *American Health*, March/April 1984

Kenton, L., and Kenton, S., *Raw Energy*, Century, London, 1984

Kenton, Leslie, *Ultrahealth*, Ebury Press, London, 1984

Salk, Jonas, *The Survival of the Wisest*, Harper & Row, New York, 1973

Chapter 3.   What is Organic Gardening?

Bohm, David, *Wholeness and the Implicate Order*, Routledge & Kegan Paul, London, 1981

Easey, Ben, *Practical Organic Gardening*, Faber & Faber, London, 1976

Hills, Lawrence, D., *Organic Gardening*, Penguin Books, London, 1977

Howard, Sir Albert, *The Soil and Health*, Schocken Books, New York, 1972 (originally published as *Farming and Gardening for Health or Disease*, Faber & Faber, London, 1965)

Larkcom, Joy, *Vegetables From Small Gardens*, Faber & Faber, London, 1976

Mayall, Sam, *Farming Organically*, Soil Association publications, 1976

Null, Gary, and Null, Steven, *Poisons in Your Body*, Arco Publishing, New York, 1977

Organic Standards Committee, *Unified Organic Standards*, Soil Association publications, 1983

Pottenger, Robert, 'Nutrition From the Ground Up', Mandala Holistic
  Health, PO Box 1233, Del Mar, CA, 92014, USA
Szekely, Edmond Bordeaux, *The Ecological Health Garden*, International
  Biogenic Society, Costa Rica, 1973
Vereijken, Dr. P., 'Research on Alternative Farming Systems in Nagele',
  Research Station for Arable Farming and Field Production of Vegetables,
  Lelystad, The Netherlands
Watson, Alexandra, 'No Future for Chemical Farming', *Soil Association
  Review*, March 1984
Woodward, Lawrence, 'Understanding the Message of the Soil', *New
  Farmer and Grower*, No.7 Summer 1985, British Organic Farmers and
  Growers, Bristol

Chapter 4.   The Gaia Hypothesis

Lovelock, James, *Gaia—A New Look At Life on Earth*, Oxford University
  Press, Oxford, 1979
Lovelock, James, 'Are We Destabilising World Climate?', *The Ecologist*,
  Vol.15 No.1/2
Lutzenberger, Jose, 'The World Bank's Polonoroeste Project: A Social and
  Environmental Catastrophe', *The Ecologist*, Vol.15 No.1/2
Rich, Bruce M., 'Multi-lateral Development Banks. Their Role in
  Destroying the Global Environment', *The Ecologist*, Vol.15 No.1/2
Roberts, M. B. V., *Biology—A Functional Approach*, Thomas Nelson &
  Sons, Surrey, 1971
Russel, Peter, *The Awakening Earth*, Ark Paperbacks, London, 1984
Samuels, Mike, and Bennett, Hal Zina, *Well Body, Well Earth*, Sierra Book
  Club, San Francisco, 1983

Chapter 5.   Eat Organic!

Hills, Lawrence, D., *Organic Gardening*, Penguin Books, London, 1977
Hodges, R. D., 'A Qualitative Comparison Between Conventional and
  Biological Husbandry', In *Biological Husbandry, A Scientific Approach to
  Organic Farming*, ed. by B. Stonehouse, Butterworths, London, 1981
Kenton, L. and Kenton, S., *Raw Energy*, Century, London, 1984
Knorr, D. and Vogtmann, H., 'Quantity and Quality Determination of
  Ecologically Grown Foods', In Knorr, D. (Ed.), *Sustainable Food
  Systems*, AVI Publishing, Westport, Connecticut, 1983
Pottenger, Robert, 'Nutrition From the Ground Up', Mandala Holistic
  Health, PO Box 1233, Del Mar, CA, 92014, USA
Price, Weston A., *Nutrition and Physical Degeneration*, Price-Pottenger
  Nutritional Foundation, La Mesa, California, 1970
Schuphan, Werner, 'Nutritional Value of Crops as Influenced by Organic
  and Inorganic Fertilizer Treatments', *Human Nutrition*, Vol.23, No.4
  1974

Samuels, Mike, and Bennett, Hal Zina, *Well Body*, *Well Earth*, Sierra Book
    Club, San Francisco, 1983
Vogtmann, Dr. Hartmut, 'The Food Quality Controversy', *Proceedings of
    the IFOAM* No.48
Vogtmann, Dr. Hartmut, 'The Quality of Agricultural Produce Originating
    from Different Systems of Cultivation', Soil Association publications,
    1981
Yellowlees, W. W., 'Ill Fares the Land' James Mackenzie Lecture, 1978,
    Journal of the Royal College of General Practitioners, Vol.29, 1979

Chapter 6.   The Quantum Link
Bohm, David, *Wholeness and the Implicate Order*, Routledge & Kegan Paul,
    London, 1980
Heisenberg, Werner, *Physics and Philosophy*, Harper Torchbooks, New
    York, 1958
Pearce, Joseph Chilton, *Magical Child Matures*, E. P. Dutton, New York,
    1985
Pelletier, Kenneth., *Towards a Science of Consciousness*, Delta Publishing,
    New York, 1978
Salk, Jonas, *The Survival of the Wisest*, Harper & Row, New York, 1973
Schlegel, R., 'Quantum Physics and Human Purpose', *Zygon*, Vol.8 No.3,
    September 1973
Schlegel, R., 'Conversation in the Afternoon', *Zygon*, Vol.7 No.4,
    December 1973

Part II.   Gaiaculture
Evans, Hazel, *The City Garden*, Futura, London, 1985
French, Jaqueline, *Organic Gardening in Australia*, Reed Books, Frenchs
    Forest NSW 2086, Australia, 1986
Fukuoka, *The One Straw Revolution*, Rodale Press, USA
Hessayon, D. G., *Vegetable Plotter*, Pan Britannica Industries, Waltham
    Cross, Herts, 1977
Hills, Lawrence, D., *Organic Gardening*, Penguin Books, London, 1977
Howard, Sir Albert, *The Soil and Health*, Schocken Books, New York, 1972
    (originally published as *Farming and Gardening for Health or Disease*,
    Faber & Faber, London, 1965)
Kenton, L., and Kenton, S., *Raw Energy*, Century, London, 1984
Kenton, Leslie, *Ultrahealth*, Ebury Press, London, 1984
Larkcom, Joy, *Vegetables From Small Gardens*, Faber & Faber, London,
    1976
Larkcom, Joy, *Salads The Year Round*, Hamlyn, Middlesex, 1980
Pears, Pauline M., *Raised Bed Gardening The Organic Way*, Henry
    Doubleday Research Association, Coventry, 1983

Riotte, Louise, *Carrots Love Tomatoes*, Garden Way Publishing, Vermont
    1975
Salter, P. J. and Bleasdale J. K. A. & others, *Know & Grow Vegetables*,
    Vol.1&2, Oxford University Press, Oxford, 1979 & 1982
Simons, Arthur J., *The New Vegetable Grower's Handbook*, Penguin Books,
    London, revised 1975
Szekely, Edmond Bordeaux, *The Ecological Health Garden*, International
    Biogenic Society, Costa Rica, 1973

Useful Addresses

Organic Organizations

The Biodynamic Agricultural Association
Woodman Lane, Clent,
Stourbridge, West Midlands
DY9 9PX
Tel. (0562) 884933
Organic gardening based on the principles of Rudolf Steiner

The Henry Doubleday Research Association
Ryton Gardens, Ryton-on-Dunsmore, Coventry CV8 3LG
Tel. (0203) 303517
The leading British association for organic gardeners. Membership includes journal, book and gardening products list. Well worth a visit

Middle Wood Centre
Roeburndale West, Wray,
Lancaster LA2 8QX
Tel. (0468) 21031/21947
120 acres of native woodland and permaculture techniques

The Soil Association
86–88 Colston Street, Bristol
BS1 5BB
Tel. (0272) 290661
Centre of organic movement in Britain. Excellent Quarterly Review and book list. Organic Products Directory

Working Weekends on Organic Farms
19 Bradford Road, Lewes, East
Sussex BN7 1RB
Enclose SAE for information

Other Organizations

Earthlife Foundation
10 Belgrave Square, London
SW1X 8PF
Tel. (01) 235 7055
Charity intent on saving Gaia's rainforests

Friends of the Earth
377 City Road, London EC1V 1NA
Tel. (01) 837 0731
Well organized information and campaigns against pesticides and environmental destruction

The London Food Commission
PO Box 291, London N5 1DU
Tel. (01) 633 5782
Pressure group concerned with the irradiation and denaturing of the food we eat

Oxfam
274 Banbury Road, Oxford
OX2 7DZ
Tel. (0865) 56777
Charity concerned with Third World development

Addresses for seeds and organic products

Betagro
Trewinnard House, Perran-ar-Worthal, Truro, Cornwall TR3 7QD
Tel. (0872) 865614
Worm worked composts

Joseph Bentley Ltd
Barrow-on-Humber, South Humberside DN19 7AQ
Tel. (Barrow-on-Humber) 30501
Nicotine, pure soft soap, and other sprays

Bio Plant Care
Pine Ridge Vineyard, Robertsbridge, E. Sussex
Bio-san to prevent fungal attacks, including blight

Biodynamic Agricultural Association
Woodman Lane, Clent, Stourbridge, West Midlands DY9 9PX
Tel. (0562) 884933
Biodynamic preparations and general information on biodynamic growing

Brome & Schimmer Ltd
Greatbridge Road Industrial Estate, Romsey, Hampshire SO5 0HR
Tel. (Romsey) 515595
Quassia

John Chambers
15 Westleigh Road, Barton Seagrave, Kettering, Northants NN15 5AJ
Tel. (0933) 681632
Unusual seeds

Chase Organics
Terminal House, Shepperton, Middlesex TW17 8AS
Tel. (0932) 221212
Seaweed products and organic seeds

Cowpact Ltd
Hollingdon, Leighton Buzzard, Bedfordshire LU7 0DN
Tel. (Soulbury) 506
Organic potting compost

Cornish Calcified Seaweed Company
Newham, Truro, Cornwall TR1 2ST
Tel. (0872) 78878
Calcified seaweed

Cumulus Organics and Conservation Ltd
Timber Yard, 2 Mile Lane, Highnam, Gloucester GL2 8BR
Tel. (0452) 305814
General organic composts and fertilizers, including rock potash; fish, blood and bone; seaweed meal

Samuel Dobie & Son Ltd
PO Box 90, Paignton, Devon TQ3 1XY
Tel. (0803) 616281
Seeds and general garden products

Donaldsons Hortopaper
Suite 15, Essex House, 15 Station Road, Upminster, Essex RM14 2SJ
Tel. (04022) 51300
Hortopaper mulch

Henry Doubleday Research Association (HDRA)
Ryton Gardens, Ryton-on-Dunsmore, Coventry CV8 3LG
Tel. (0203) 303517
Burgundy mixture, and a wide range of organic pest control, green manures etc

Thomas Elliot Ltd
Hast Hill, Baston Manor Road, Hayes, Bromley, Kent BR2 7AJ
Tel. (01) 462 1207
Potting compost

Fertosan Products Ltd
2 Holborn Square, Lower Tranmere, Birkenhead, Merseyside L41 9HQ
Tel. (051) 647 5041
Fertosan slug destroyer

Humber Fertilizers plc
PO Box 27, Stoneferry, Hull HU8 8DQ
Tel. (Hull) 20458
Organic compost

A. W. Maskell & Sons Ltd
Dirleton Works, Stephenson Street, Canning Town, London E16 4SA
Tel. (01) 476 6321
Fish meal

Maxicrop Ltd
21 London Road, Great Shelford, Cambridge CB2 5DF
Tel. (0223) 844024
Seaweed products

Joseph Metcalf Ltd
Brookside Lane, Oswaldtwistle, Accrington, Lancs BB5 3NY
Tel. (0254) 393321
Fish meal

Sea Trident Ltd
Sarum House, Oak Park, Dawlish, Devon EX7 0DE
Tel. (0626) 862489
Seaweed products, rock phosphate

The Solar Quest
Applegreen Lodge, Bossington Lane, Porlock, Minehead, Somerset TA24 8HD
Tel. (0643) 862939
Homeopathic preparations

Suffolk Herbs
Sawyers Farm, Little Cornard, Sudbury, Suffolk CO10 0NY
Tel. (0787) 227247
Herb and vegetable seeds, green manures, seaweed meal, and other products

Synchemicals Ltd
44 Grange Walk, London SE1 3EN
Tel. (01) 237 1958/9
Nicotine

Cloche Suppliers

Agriframes Ltd
Charlwoods Road, East Grinstead, West Sussex RH19 29G
Tel. (0342) 28644
Floating film and general polythene film and netting

Samuel Dobie & Son Ltd
PO Box 90, Paignton, Devon TQ3 1XY
Tel. (0803) 616281
Corrugated PVC cloches, general garden seeds and hardware

LBS Polythene
Standroyd Mill, Cottontree, Colne,
Lancs BB8 7BB
Tel. (0282) 862200
General polythene products

Stewart Garden Products
Purley Way, Croydon CR9 4HS
Polypropylene cloches, seedtrays, and pots

Westray Cloches
15 Church Road, Upper
Boddington, Daventry,
Northampton NN11 6DL
Tel. (0327) 60329
Cloches

Conversion tables between metric and imperial measurement

Inches to centimetres

1in = 2.5cm
2in = 5cm
3in = 7.5cm
4in = 10cm
5in = 12.5cm
6in = 15cm
7in = 17.5cm
8in = 20cm

9in = 22.5cm
10in = 25cm
11in = 27.5cm
12in = 30cm
18in = 45cm
24in = 60cm
30in = 75cm
36in = 90cm

Weight

1oz = 25g
1g = 0.04oz
1lb = 0.45kg
1kg = 2.2lb
1cwt= 50.8kg
1kg = 0.02cwt

Temperature

°C	−20	−10	0	10	20	37
°F	−4		14	32	50	68	98.6

Volume (UK measures)

1fl oz = 25ml   1ml   = 0.04fl oz
1pt   = 0.57 litre 1 litre = 1.76pts
1gal   = 4.55 litres 1 litre = 0.22gal
(NB: 1 UK pint = 20fl oz, 1 USA pint = 18fl oz)

Index